The Anthropological Paradox

This book addresses how the erosion of traditional forms of political association and legal regulation has given rise to a pluralism of "imperfect communities" constantly exposed to the risk of dissolution. These are niches and micro-worlds that are connected through precarious and ambivalent ties. Such a far-reaching transformation affects at one and the same time both our psychic and social identity. The book argues that this phenomenon is linked to the proliferation of new forms of psychic "disorder" – depression, personality disorder, dissociation – typical of hypermodern societies. However, while these can easily turn into genuine disorders, they can also open onto richer forms of identity, more complex than those of the past. Based on this analysis, the book's main claim is that this dynamic epitomizes a general anthropological paradox – one that has always marked the human animal: humans are bound by their own biological constitution to fend off disorder by drawing the boundaries of artificial niches, and yet they are inclined to expose themselves to unlimited contingency so that they can find a truly suitable environment.

Pursuing a novel understanding of the apparent collapse of traditional juridico-political settings, this book makes the case that the emergence of dissociations at several levels – individual, social, political, legal – does not stem from a lack of political imagination. Rather, it is a situation with which humans are inevitably confronted: a perennial tension between the limited and the unlimited, between the desire to take refuge and the desire to cross borders.

Massimo De Carolis is Full Professor of Political Philosophy and Social Philosophy at the University of Salerno, where he is the head of the Laboratory of Studies and Research on Human Nature. Among his most recent books are *La vita nell'epoca della sua riproducibilità tecnica* (*Life in the Age of its Technological Reproducibility*, 2004), and *Il rovescio della libertà. Tramonto del neoliberalismo e disagio della civiltà* (*The Downside of Freedom. The Twilight of Neoliberalism and Civilization's Discontent*, 2017).

Law and Politics, Continental Perspectives

Series Editors
Mariano Croce, *Sapienza University of Rome, Italy*
Marco Goldoni, *University of Glasgow, UK*

For information about the series and details of previous and forthcoming titles, see https://www.routledge.com/law/series/LPCP

A GlassHouse book

The Anthropological Paradox

Niches, Micro-worlds and Psychic Dissociation

Massimo De Carolis

Routledge
Taylor & Francis Group
LONDON AND NEW YORK

First published 2018 by Routledge

2 Park Square, Milton Park, Abingdon, Oxfordshire OX14 4RN
52 Vanderbilt Avenue, New York, NY 10017

Routledge is an imprint of the Taylor & Francis Group, an informa business

First issued in paperback 2019

Translated by Richard Bates

Published in Italian as Il paradosso antropologico. Nicchie, micromondi e dissociazione psichica by Quodlibet 2008

British Library Cataloguing in Publication Data
A catalogue record for this book is available from the British Library

Library of Congress Cataloging in Publication Data
Names: De Carolis, Massimo, 1954- author. | Translation of: De Carolis, Massimo, 1954- Paradosso antropologico.
Title: The anthropological paradox / Massimo De Carolis.
Other titles: Paradosso antropologico. English
Description: New York : Routledge, 2018. | Series: Law and politics: Continental perspectives | "Published in Italian as Il paradosso antropologico. Nicchie, micromondi e dissociazione psichica by Quodlibet 2008." | Includes bibliographical references and index.
Identifiers: LCCN 2017048663 (print) | LCCN 2017049777 (ebook) | ISBN 9781351137546 (ebk) | ISBN 9781138281035 (hbk : alk. paper)
Subjects: LCSH: Philosophical anthropology.
Classification: LCC BD450 (ebook) | LCC BD450 .D349313 2018 (print) | DDC 128—dc23
LC record available at https://lccn.loc.gov/2017048663

ISBN: 978-1-138-28103-5 (hbk)
ISBN: 978-0-367-34892-2 (pbk)

Typeset in Galliard
by Taylor & Francis Books

Contents

Preface to the English edition

Niches and imperfect communities

I

The Anthropological Paradox is an attempt to reflect on the relation between the present political situation and what, with only the slightest emphasis, may be called *human nature*. I mean by this term all those generically human demands, needs or desires, which we can reasonably interpret as so many clues, symptoms or reflexes of a constitution that is shared by *all* members of our species, although their particular manifestations can only emerge from time to time in the course of a specific life. Isolating the generically human component in each case and distinguishing it from its contingent variations is certainly a bold enterprise – one that entails the risk of error and subjective illusion. It does not, however, seem a task one may opt out of, given that, in practice, there has never been a human culture that has not planned its own *particular* forms of life on the basis of some more or less reliable image of human existence *in general*.

Human nature, by definition, does not change unless imperceptibly in the course of history. What *can* change, though, is the *image* of the human condition on which individual and collective life is based in one age or another. What most certainly changes are the political institutions and the forms of social organization in which the generically human demands are required to express themselves, so that they may be translated into stable, rewarding forms of existence. Changes of this kind can sometimes be so swift and profound as to oblige us to rethink not only the existential strategies to which we entrust our lives, but also the very idea of our humanity that underpins these strategies. The underlying hypothesis of the book is that a radical change of this kind has been taking place over the last few decades, and that the social, political and philosophical theories available to us are still struggling to grasp (and even find words for) the ongoing change.

To take the measure of this change fully, it may be useful to step back a moment and look at a classic of ancient thought: Aristotle's treatise on *Politics*, whose opening remarks describe the *polis* as a *perfect* community[1] – which does not mean that the City-State is without its limitations or defects. The sense is that it is a

1 Koinonia teleios polis (*Pol.*, 1252b28).

collective organization, complete in itself, unrelated to anything else, that "achieves, so to speak, the limit of perfect autarky (self-sufficiency and self-determination)". Hence the initially disconcerting deduction that a political community is such *by nature*.[2] Here too we must move with caution if we are not to misinterpret the text. The *polis* is certainly not a "natural" given, as old and widespread as man. In various other passages, in fact, Aristotle shows clearly that, in his view, a *perfect* community is a late and decidedly rare fruit of historical development. The autarkic organization of the *polis* has, however, an ideal relation with *human* nature as "man is a political animal and naturally tends to share his life" (1169b 18). Only a *perfect* political community – autonomous to the point of autarky – can offer a truly satisfying response to the generically human tendency to seek a happy, shared life.

Imperfect forms of sharing can be found everywhere in social life, and in his meditations on friendship Aristotle underlines how varied and heterogeneous they are: there is sharing between spouses, between parents and children, between members of the same clan, as there is between comrades in arms or even simple fellow travellers. Each partial and relative form of community has its own specific way of uniting, making "friends", and thus offering protection and a place of retreat. However, none of these *imperfect communities* can adequately express the "political nature" of our species, for the simple reason that what is being shared, in each case, is some specific interest or aim, and never *life as such*. By contrast, real political action is not limited to administering interests and objectives held in common, but sets up a kind of sharing that is much more profound and, above all, much more deeply rooted in the absolute uniqueness of the human condition. The citizens of a *polis* are required to respond together (in practice and not just in theory) to the most basic of existential questions: *how* do we intend to live? On what priorities and values do we intend to build our collective existence? What form is, for us, the *true* form of a life that is suited to our humanity?

Clearly, questions of this kind would have no sense for any other living species, whatever their degree of natural sociality. The lion, the bee and the wolf have just *one* form of life, just one *bios*, deposited from the start in the instincts with which each individual creature is endowed. Only the human species seems to have such a high degree of flexibility and contingency as to make it at least reasonable to reflect that "the carpenter and the cobbler have certain characteristic actions and activities, and a human being has none".[3] In our case, in short, the form of life is, at least partly, an open question, a gap to be filled, which requires an absolutely special kind of collective practice: which is precisely what is at stake in *politics*.

In Aristotle, and ancient thought generally, the idea of any open and problematic nature in the human species is barely hinted at. Only in the modern world has this kind of anthropological intuition acquired decisive philosophical and political weight. For example, the passage from Pico della Mirandola quoted in the epigraph

2 Pasa polis physei estin (*Pol.*, 1252b30).
3 *Eth. Nic.* I, 1097b.

to Chapter 1 of this book demonstrates with great literary power how far the modern conception of "human dignity" rested from the start on the idea of a human nature that was intimately undefined and flexible. Adam is presented as the only living being called on to plan his identity *for himself* and to give form, freely and creatively, to his life and his world. A few centuries later, Kant would appeal to the same conception to open the way to cosmopolitanism, recalling that human actions are not exhausted in the mere achievement of some more or less useful end, but have the much deeper and more elusive task of "fill[ing] the void in creation as regards their goal" (Kant 1784, A393). In twentieth-century German philosophical anthropology a similar conception of the human would be translated into a coherent, detailed line of research.

The more the open, auto-poietic character of human nature comes to the fore, the more logical it is that any enquiry into the "ideal" community, able to tackle more completely the task of creatively giving form to the collective life, becomes more radical. It is therefore understandable that modern culture should return to and emphasize the distinction in rank between the *perfect* community (that is now the only recognized legitimate political subject) and the partial, imperfect forms of sharing that can proliferate within it. The sharp opposition in Hobbes and other writers between *people* and *multitude* not only repeats this distinction, but circumscribes more closely the idea of a "perfect" community, associating Aristotle's criterion of self-sufficiency with that of *homogeneousness*. The "people" is now a source of legitimate sovereignty only if it can speak with a single voice, act as a single person, and *merge* its internal differences in a single identity – the diametrical opposite of a heterogeneous and plural multitude. Thus, in the modern age *forging a people* as a prototype of the "perfect" community became not only the one really decisive political action, but even the basic premise of *civilization* in the broadest sense of the term.

Logically, this kind of fusion of the "many" in a single subject would be all the easier to achieve the more it could rest on a network of pre-conditions, such as a shared language, cultural tradition, or more or less homogeneous ethnic group. This explains why the nation-state rapidly became the prototype of the modern idea of a "perfect" community in Europe. Clearly, however, a "nation" or "people", in the modern sense, can never become simply a natural state of affairs that has been acquired once and for all. Self-determination, unity and homogeneousness are the result of tenaciously constant government action that involves risk and conflict, and that has an inevitable *cost*. During the period of late modernity, as social complexity has gradually increased, that cost has gone on rising.[4]

4 Carl Schmitt, more than any other twentieth-century thinker, insisted on the need to keep firm, at all costs, the sovereignty of the state and the homogeneousness of a people. His support of Nazism can therefore stand as a forceful example of how much in the meantime the political cost had increased of maintaining an order that, by Schmitt's own explicit admission, required, "if necessary, the exclusion or elimination of the heterogeneous" (Schmitt 1926, p. 94).

This long preamble was necessary to take the full measure of the historical fracture that we have been witnessing in this period. Given these premises, we can define as *hypermodern* a type of society in which no *perfect* community seems able to take form any longer, if not at such an exorbitant cost as to discredit from the start any political project that gave real (and not just verbal) support to the need for it. A society, then, in which only *imperfect* communities can exist, often able to provide protection and a retreat, and sometimes designed to inspire the deepest loyalty, but marked in every case by their external *dependence* and their internal *heterogeneousness* – a world of *niches*, rather than peoples and nations.

Presumably, a situation of this kind will force us to rethink from top to bottom the very idea of a civil order, but this is not the only problem left open. If, as Aristotle implies, it is the desire to share *life as such* that drives us towards a perfect community, what is left of that desire in a hypermodern society? How can the generically human need to give a complete form to one's life be expressed in a world of niches? To "fill the void in creation" as regards the meaning of human life? These, essentially, are the questions this book addresses.

2

I have a logical reason for preferring the term "hypermodern" to "postmodern", which enjoyed such popularity in the European debate a few decades ago. In effect, I find it misleading to think of two models of a social order that are wholly autonomous and distinct, and that succeeded each other in time, following a logic of before and after. In actual fact, the model I am suggesting we call "hypermodern" has played its role on the stage of modernity from the start, though its position has been marginal, unacknowledged or openly polemical towards the institutional paradigm founded on the idea of *legitimate sovereignty* that was eventually to impose itself as the prototype of modernity.

As we have seen, in the idea of modernity that has guided European history, everything revolves around a *horizontal split* that sharply separates an above and a below. Above, in sovereign position, is the legitimate power representing the unity of the people, usually identified with the nation-state; below, in subaltern position, family clans and religious groupings, leagues and the other imperfect communities that populate the multitude. However, as soon as we start scratching the surface, we find there is no period of modern history that does not allude, at least in passing, to an alternative model. Here the seat of sovereign power remains unoccupied – or is consigned to a remote, unknowable, metaphysical entity – and the imperfect communities are called on to construct the social order through some alliance with each other. The structure that emerges therefore resembles a network of *vertical splits*, which distinguish incomplete groups and segments, driven to coordinate and cooperate with each other, not to merge in a single subject, but to preserve their specific identity and their autonomy.

In the first centuries of modernity, the traces of an alternative model of this kind seem more marked in those contexts furthest away from the creation of a national state: in the Florence of Pico and Machiavelli, for example, or in the United Provinces that formed the background to Spinoza's ethical-political meditations. In advanced modernity, by contrast, the great social experiment that was meanwhile taking form on American soil soon became the chosen ground for the clash of the two paradigms of civil order that I have just distinguished. The forms of mass immigration inevitably involved a scaling down of the ties of national (as well as religious, ethnic and other) affiliation, and this wholly new situation authorized two opposing reactions. The Latin motto *E pluribus unum* or the metaphor of the *melting pot* still allude to the need to merge the multitude into a single subject and, therefore, a "perfect" community of continental dimensions. The *political pluralism* current in the most advanced liberal circles, by contrast, clearly proceeds in the direction of a "hypermodern" order that recognizes America as a "nation of nations", excludes any form of hegemony or discrimination, and favours the formation of a "majority of minorities", in which the various interest groups and partial communities overlap and mutually recognize each other.[5]

In the 1980s, under the drive of neo-liberalism, it began to seem that the hypermodern model must inevitably be extended to the whole planet, almost without any significant resistance. Hence the widespread conviction in those years that modernity was literally passing away, to open the gates to a completely new age. A few decades later, however, the neo-liberal project of a "new global order" seemed clearly in crisis, while in every geopolitical area, appeals to the unity of the people and sovereignty were thriving, presented again, exactly as in Hobbes, as the only antidote to disorder and universal conflict. Finding a way out of an impasse like this is a task of enormous proportions, for which we are not in the least prepared. I believe, however, that, if we are to take stock of the contemporary world, it is crucial to recognize that the problem does not concern just the political and social dimensions, but also that of the *psychic* identity of individual subjects.

In the classical paradigm of modernity, the horizontal split between above and below does not actually define just the ideal model of the political community, but also that of a healthy, ordered and civil *psychic* identity, in which the Ego keeps under control the partial, multiform drives that agitate the Id, just as a sovereign subdues the uprisings of the multitude. It is no mere formal analogy, but a necessary parallelism. To construct *civilization* in the modern sense of the term requires more than just devising the most appropriate social mechanisms. We also need to produce a *type of person* who is adaptable to these mechanisms and able to ensure their reproduction. In short, we are speaking of a complex form of anthropotechnics that must simultaneously mobilize both social and psychic dynamics.

One may logically suppose, then, that the hypermodern fracture is spreading in both the inner and outer world; that it is not merely heading towards a different social order, but also towards a different type of psychic economy. To be still more

5 The formula "majority of minorities" was coined by Robert A. Dahl in the 1950s, at the same time as the first models of "overlapping consensus", a formula that was later to become, particularly thanks to Rawls, the basic principle of political liberalism.

precise, the underlying hypothesis of this book is that the current change is rooted in what sociologists call the *interpenetration* of the social and psychic spheres: the complex, elusive terrain on which the two dimensions appropriate each other, becoming indistinguishable. Our greatest difficulty on the scientific level is that the most respected theories in recent years have treated this kind of terrain as a no man's land, ignoring or repressing it, when not openly questioning its existence.

A superficial overview may give us an idea of how the difficulty is re-expressed in absolutely similar terms, both in research on the psychic system and in analysis of social phenomena; and of how, in both fields, the root of the problem is older and deeper than might appear at first sight. The "naturalization of the mind", for example, promoted in this period by experimental psychology and the neurosciences, deliberately treats the psychic system as a closed entity, abstractly separated from any interaction with the social and communications spheres. However, this is not an isolated extreme or a recent trend: one need only consider that even the basic concepts of psychoanalysis, at least in their canonical formulation, do not entail any structural interconnection between psychic and social dynamics. Yet, everything suggests that, in the last few decades, the *actual* forms of psychic distress have been developing in the *opposite* direction from that proposed by the theories. It is, in fact, more and more difficult to play down or deny the role of the social dimension on typically hypermodern phenomena, such as rampant depression or the growing number of dissociative inclinations.[6] However, although there has been growing discord between facts and theories in this respect, at the moment there seems to be no sign of a change of direction. More and more often, one has the impression that the theories are going round in circles, leaving individual psychiatrists or counsellors the task of dealing with the emergency.

For their part, the social sciences present a fairly similar picture. Niklas Luhmann's theory of social systems, for example, though it includes the concept of "interpenetration" in its major categories, actually deals with social systems as closed worlds with their own autonomous logics, on which human desires and intentions can have, on principle, only an indirect and minimal bearing. On the other hand, the tendency to minimize or exclude the "human factor" from statistical calculation and the control of social dynamics is much older, and its citadel is the one social science that has long been regarded as mathematically precise: *economics*. The main concern of mainstream economists in recent years has been gradually to neutralize "psychological" factors that still had a significant role in theories that were certainly not naive, like those of John Maynard Keynes: radical uncertainty, confidence and the role of long-term expectations. The collective effort has thus given birth to an arsenal of algorithms and systems of calculation that are perfectly "scientific": not only lacking any reference to the psychic dimension, but deliberately *blind* to this dimension. As a result, they were so widespread in the financial

6 On the interconnection between the psychic and social planes in the most widespread present-day forms of psychic disturbance, see Ehrenberg (1998) and Benasayag and Schmit (2003).

community that they contributed in no small measure to the explosion of the great crisis in 2008.

Such a huge impasse cannot be unblocked by the application of psychological concepts to social analyses and vice versa. Instead, we must get used to the idea that constructing psychic identity and constructing a collective social order are not two distinct processes – perhaps with occasional points of contact – but the two poles of a *single* dynamic, in which human life takes specific forms, and where what is at stake is no less than what we usually refer to by the term "civilization"; that we may need to resign ourselves to the idea that the exploration of such a profound anthropological terrain will inevitably come up against paradoxes, vicious circles and margins of uncertainty that cannot always be dealt with in the traditional frame of reference of scientific discourse.

This, in short, is the intellectual horizon of the various intertwined strands in this work: the analysis of dissociative phenomena; the extension of the concept of "vertical splitting" to social dynamics; and a critical consideration of early twentieth-century German philosophical anthropology. Now that a few years have gone by since it was first published, I hope that an unprejudiced reader will quickly recognize the urgency and the objective difficulties of the project, while registering the relative haste and shortcomings that a work of speculation must inevitably allow for. What I would like to do now is use the short remaining space of this preface to bring into sharper focus the concept of "imperfect community", which is the fruit of more recent research,[7] but which, I believe, may also help to clarify the project that even then lay behind this work.

3

Actually, the expression "imperfect community" does not come from political theory, but from *logic*. What is called the "problem of the imperfect community" is raised by *sets* that are antithetical to *natural* classes. These are heterogeneous classes, whose members do not necessarily share a structural feature or objective similarity, but are associated *conventionally* by the logical operation that classifies them together (a canonical example being the sun, the number three, the First World War and Groucho Marx, which are associated by the mere property of appearing in the above list). Logical considerations of this kind obviously do not remove the banal fact of resemblances between things. They show, however, that, as the possible resemblances and possible criteria of classification are innumerable, none of them is, strictly speaking, more or less "natural" than any other: any criterion is equally legitimate and any community equally relative, contingent and, indeed, *imperfect*.[8]

7 See De Carolis (2017).

8 Much of the credit for starting the debate on the "problem of the imperfect community" goes to Goodman (1951, 1956).

What makes the question politically significant is the fact that a hypermodern, pluralist and virtually global society will naturally tend to generate similarly heterogeneous, partial groups, united each time by a convergence that, however fortuitous, may nevertheless be translated, in certain conditions, into an effective political machine. For example, one typical feature of movements often wrongly defined as "populist" is their heterogeneous nature. In Argentina a few decades ago Peronists of left and right coexisted, conservatives and revolutionaries, associated in practice almost exclusively by their declaration of loyalty to their leader. Just as in the example from logic, the community tie in these cases is created by an act of pure convention, with no reference to any presupposed "natural" affinity. The apparently arbitrary nature of the operation is much reduced if we consider that similar movements are usually born as a reaction to what is perceived as a degeneration of social life, which is assimilated to a system of closed, privileged *castes* to the detriment of the man in the street. This means that *not* belonging to one caste or the other – simply being "an ordinary person" – may be claimed as a positive pre-condition of asking for and receiving *trust*.

In this respect at least, such heterogeneous groups, in the end, are not substantially different from those typical of *minorities*, though for the latter the decisive factor seems to be precisely a shared quality that is clear and unequivocal, and sometimes *natural* in the most direct sense: being black, homosexual, Muslim or French-Canadian. Here too, what essentially binds the community together is the need for *trust*. An immigrant in a foreign country usually *entrusts* himself to his fellow countrymen, and all of us tend to *trust* and have *confidence* in those who share the existential choices we think most valuable.

Trust is clearly a subjective factor that cannot be imposed to order and which may, for logical reasons, fluctuate significantly. Each member of an imperfect community possesses innumerable attributes and is therefore, at least virtually, the possible member of innumerable *other* communities. He will never be simply "an ordinary person", unless a conventional choice somehow puts his positive properties "in brackets". In any case, mutual trust and group cohesion will be transferred to conventions of this kind, which are all the more unstable and precarious, the higher the level of social complexity.

If it wants political weight, the group must, then, reinforce the *loyalty* of its members and avert any risk of its betrayal with all the more force, the more fragile is the tie that binds them. In other words, it must ensure that, at least subjectively, the community tie is equivalent to the "sharing of life itself", though, strictly speaking, an equivalence of that kind can be no more than an expedient, a conventional construct. In this way the interconnected concepts of trust, loyalty and confidence (in many languages *all* these terms derive ultimately from the Latin *fides*) end up delineating the outlines of a protective niche, reinforced by expectations and bonds of specific loyalties, and distinct from the rest of the social dynamic. This dimension – both psychic and social – is now the one in which the drive to "share life" of which Aristotle spoke is best expressed. It should not surprise us, then, if we also find in the imperfect communities of the present traces of the *negative* and *problematic* component of this drive: indeterminacy, the "void in creation", with all the difficulties that attend it on the political plane.

Let us not forget that an imperfect community, by definition, is part of a vaster social dynamic, from which it has no way of breaking free. It is therefore logical to suppose that it is formed halfway between two contrary drives. The first, which I have just referred to, is the drive "from below", which moves all those who, for one reason or another, are seeking someone they can trust. However, in the nature of things, there is also a drive "from above", exercised by the networks of government and control of society as a whole, which tends to intercept, classify and capture any kind of emerging community, if only to ensure that its criteria of internal loyalty do not collide with the general rules of conduct and public order.

Since modern police techniques have appeared, the control of emerging communities has, in effect, always followed an underlying principle, whose logic is apparently incontestable. It has been thought desirable to discourage and, where necessary, repress *political* communities that are united by a shared *general* project of civil order that, in an emergency, might threaten the constituted order in its given form. At the same time groups that are united by a *particular* interest have been tolerated and sometimes openly encouraged, once it is clear that this interest could be included in the conventions that are in force and so become part of the constituted order and a further support to it. In this respect, the techniques of government developed by neo-liberalism are indistinguishable from traditional systems of control, apart from one important aspect: the emerging groups are regarded as more or less compatible with the overall social order, not so much for any declarations of loyalty to the sovereign, the nation or the unity of the people, as for their adherence to the mechanisms of the market, and the economic and legal conventions that regulate their dynamics. In other words, an imperfect community is recognized and protected as a piece in the jigsaw of society as a whole, if it is committed to pursuing its ends in the forms of negotiation of which the market is the paradigm, adapting to the procedures that regulate competition and respecting their verdict each time.

Clearly, the idea is that market forces (extended and strengthened by technology) can contain social antagonism within the conventional, regulated framework of competition. They would actually drive the different communities – interdependent although they are rivals – to enforced cooperation and mutual recognition. This détente would neutralize the spectre of a "war of all against all", as any escalation of *absolute* conflict would be less and less worthwhile and therefore less probable, even though the complex and costly spectacle of legitimation that necessarily accompanied the constituting of sovereign power in the "classical" paradigm of modernity would be reduced to a minimum.

These are the principles with which liberal democracies in recent decades have faced the development of multiculturalism and, more generally, the demands for recognition coming from the various communities they contain. On the one hand, they try to *de-politicize* the various groups, driving them to put aside any projects for a general redefinition of the civil order, which, in still quite recent times, were what held together the most incisive social movements. At the same time they encourage their full recognition as *niche* subjects, with their special preferences, in a market economy.[9] At a decidedly higher level of intensity, the same logic has been applied to the attempts at nation building following a military occupation, as in the cases of Iraq and Libya.

In both cases the balance sheet of the operation seems decidedly discouraging at the moment. The de-politicization of the various groups has not led to any real reduction in conflict, at least not to the extent that was hoped for. On the contrary, the most acute crises even seem to reawaken the ghost of a "global civil war", something evoked for the first time by Carl Schmitt more than half a century ago. Not only that: the growing lack of distinction between the political and economic planes seems to encourage the genesis of new centres of power, elusive and unprincipled, protagonists of a growing process of *re-feudalizing* society. Clearly, this is not the place for a systematic consideration of the failures of neo-liberalism. All that matters is to understand how far the highly paradoxical interconnection of the psychic and social dimensions can throw light on a situation of this kind, and, in particular, on the internal dynamics of imperfect communities, which are the main actors in it.

4

Sooner or later, an imperfect community, which claims to provide an answer to the generically human demands of its members, is inevitably faced with an alternative. It can deny and conceal its imperfection, acting as if it were more complete and homogeneous than it really is, and possibly paying a price for its systematic disavowal of reality. Or it can claim its imperfection as an exemplary feature of the human condition, as a pre-condition for openness to the world and for the creative construction of its identity.

In specific individual cases the two options often coexist in a paradoxical hybrid. Sooner or later, however, one horn of the dilemma or the other is likely to prove stronger. The long-distance nationalists described by Benedict Anderson – now sometimes transformed into "sleeping cells" of international terrorism – can be taken as an extreme example of the first alternative, while the protagonists of the "creative democracy" proposed by John Dewey best exemplify the second. These two figures are presented in the last chapter of the book as ideal, conflicting examples. We still do not fully understand how far, whatever the intentions and declarations of principle, government technologies in recent years may have assisted the *first* of the two options at the expense of the second.

It is easy to understand, first of all, that a radical pluralism like that evoked by Dewey cannot fail to be part of a virtually unlimited political plan, a project concerning the whole world: *cosmo-political* in the literal sense of the term. In a perspective of this kind, adherence to the community one belongs to and its

9 See Malik (2013).

specific principles and ends, has no value in itself, but only as an example, as a contingent mirror of the indeterminacy that marks *any* form of human life, imposing the same existential burden on all to "fill the void in creation". For this reason, declaring one's loyalty is, first of all, a response to this "empty place", and only secondarily to the model of life that fills it. In some respects the logic is similar to that of the religious mystic, whose object of devotion is the god that, by definition, remains equally unknown in *all* its revelations. With the addition that in political pluralism this negative dialectic is translated into a *dual loyalty*: both to one's contingent community and to the cosmic dimension in which this specific contingency is implicitly stripped of all its privileges. This kind of dual loyalty is what, in the best cases, communities in exile aspire to. It can lead someone like Byron, for example, to die at Missolonghi, fighting for Greek independence. In these cases *political* action is the logical outcome of a vaguely paradoxical exercise in "successful dissociation".

The kind of *de-politicization* followed in recent years by the administrative system is not just an obstacle to action of this kind: it is its complete antithesis. Administrative calculations modelled on market forces recognize value only in business efficiency, in targets reached or set out, in subjective aims that make a social subject more or less competitive in relation to other groups. The "empty space" that these aims are required to fill is wholly irrelevant here, and any "cosmopolitan" plan for global order is shelved or, at best, reserved for the administrative system, which usually demands a monopoly over it, while evading any real legitimating procedure. Value, prestige and recognition will therefore tend to reward the groups best fitted to present themselves as a homogeneous, compact and self-sufficient body – in short, those most willing to act out a semblance of perfection.

In the real world, obviously, imperfect communities remain such, and must therefore *negotiate* the conditions of their existence with society overall. However, it is by no means a foregone conclusion that this kind of dependence will reduce the tendency to conflict. Inside every "niche", as we have already indicated, acting out perfection means producing a strained equivalence between the bond of the community and the sharing of life as such. Certain attributes, shared rules, traditions (often very recent, arbitrary or wholly fictitious) must serve, subjectively, as symbols of human dignity in general. Technically, we can say that they must acquire the value of a *fetish*: only in this way can they seal the bond of loyalty and trust, effectively averting any possibility of betrayal.

Which forms of leadership, propaganda or seduction carry out the operation is not, in the end, important. What counts is that the *negotiating* capacity of the group is in no way thwarted by a fetishism of this kind, but is actually enormously increased by it. Those who identify their symbols with human dignity as such will also be readily *outraged* when they see them compromised, and will therefore not hesitate to defend them, even at the cost of deploying the ultimate possibility of an *absolute* conflict. This kind of willingness to fight is not merely an ideal way of binding together a community closed in on itself; it is also a very powerful *strategic* factor, which gives immediate political credit and decisive negotiating power to whoever can mobilize it in his support. In a political arena that is more and more bound up with the competitive dynamics of the market, the emerging centres of power are unlikely to turn their backs on such a valuable opportunity.

In contrast to even the quite recent past, emerging social subjects today do not bind their identity to the project of a new world order. On the contrary, they usually tend to avoid the cosmo-political dimension, even at the cost of disavowing reality so blatantly as to reproduce exactly the psychic defence mechanism that Freud evoked in his remarks on fetishism. In this elementary sense, ours is a "de-politicized" world. However, it is a de-politicization that does not reduce dangers and conflicts, but actually risks making them worse.

The responsibility for such a disquieting situation does not lie, I believe, with neo-liberal government techniques. In the past, the most radical political movements planned to build a *counter-power* able to balance and combat the economic and political hegemony of the new centres of control in society, and certainly not just to sit at the top table in distributing power. If the project ran aground, it was not so much due to the reactions it created, as to its unresolved limitations and its internal opacity. The most ambitious aim of the project was, in any case, the creation of a possible cosmo-political alliance between the imperfect communities, able to give voice to what we might call *the demand by the governed for autonomy*. So it is by thinking about these communities, in such a way as to make evident their paradoxical logic, that we should begin to recast our understanding of contemporary society and the political order.

Introduction

This book originated in the meeting of two ideas, or hypotheses, that are decidedly disparate in both range and subject. One aims to shed light on an aspect of the human condition in general that has been rooted in it since our species was first biologically constituted. The other is restricted to contemporary society, and my analysis concentrates on some typical features of the period that reveal the gulf separating present-day forms of life from those typical of modern Europe until just a few decades ago.

Though they developed fairly independently, the two hypotheses ended up running into each other during the work, until it seemed clear that each was inseparably bound to the other, and that only by considering them together could I grasp the sense of either. Actually, this process of synthesis left only the slightest traces in the final draft, and the two hypotheses are presented from the outset as articulations of a single line of thought. The reader should therefore be able to grasp the overall sense of the book from the start, and accept or reject *in toto* its theoretical approach. However, this also means that the individual problems and difficulties that have marked the various phases of the work risk remaining in the shadows – the uncertainty of some of the solutions suggested and the questions that remain unanswered at the end, aspects that can be the liveliest features of a work of speculation. That is why the most honest way of introducing the book is to briefly set out each of its underlying themes, indicating why they have been brought together, even at the cost of revealing the patching and stitching that have been necessary, as well as possible dangling threads.

The first idea, which gave the book its title, is that the human condition is deeply marked by the paradoxical combination of two opposing, yet inseparable, demands. On the one hand, we are exposed to endless contingency, and our biological constitution gives us access to it so as to exploit its extraordinary creative potentialities. However, at the same time, we must protect ourselves from the uncertainty and danger of this unlimited contingency, carving out a circumscribed sphere of rules and symbolic values – a kind of cultural niche, distinct from the rest of the world and resistant to the indefinite multiplication of possibilities.

I say "paradox", rather than opposition, because, however antithetical the two demands are, each feeds into and reproduces from the other. The construction of a symbolic order – separated from indistinct potentiality – is actually a creative act that needs to draw on those very potentialities that it resists, and must include unlimited contingency, negativity and chaos within the order that has been called on to oppose them, if that order is not to collapse. Equally, the only way to appropriate external contingency is to clothe it in the categories and symbols whose limitations its very existence denounces and of which it is the absolute negation. This means that the very same forces that are trying to solve the paradox on the surface are reproducing it deep down. This makes it, at least in principle, insoluble. Even without eliminating it, though, we can neutralize its destructive potential, to the point of making it the premise for the stability both of the collective institutions and the psychic identity of individuals. The book seeks to define the general, hypothetical terms and conditions that decide the success or failure of this delicate operation.

Logically, there are endless possible strategies for dealing with the paradox, and each of them reflects the context, the immediate factors and the balance of forces that are pressing on a culture, a form of life, or even just an extemporary decision. That is why I have developed this general hypothesis by considering specific, highly varied thematic cruxes: from forms of psychic dissociation to ancient cosmological rituals, from the incidence of information technology on social networks to the overlapping of geographical and symbolic confines in the modern geopolitical order. At first sight they may seem anomalous and incoherent, but their apparent irrationality tends to dissolve as soon as one reads them as reflections of the anthropological paradox. This does not mean that I am proposing a unified schema or some theory that will be valid for all cases. I have simply tried to deduce from these fragmentary illustrations some plausible methodological criteria. The first is that a response to the anthropological paradox usually mobilizes and is related to both psychic and social energies. It can therefore only be reconstructed if we consider the specific resonance of both the individual and collective aspects, without naively splitting and isolating what Hegel rightly called the subjective and objective forms of the "*Geist*". Second, we do well to recall that, however stable and effective any response to the paradox may be, it will always be partial and uncertain, as one of our premises is that the paradoxical nature of the human condition is in any case bound to be perpetuated. Contradictions and fractures in a cultural model do not always indicate its limitations, then: they may sometimes actually determine its strength. In any case, this latent paradox usually defines a blind spot that will inevitably remain invisible to give stability to our visual field. No cultural practice can really delude itself that it can see this blind spot, and for this very reason there is a margin of inevitable illusion in any cognitive act. It is a warning we should not forget, as science and philosophy are themselves not only theories, but attempts to deal with the paradox.

I am not, of course, claiming that these ideas are wholly new. In a sense, it would be somewhat alarming if they were, given that the most reliable confirmation of an anthropological approach is that it leaves its traces in a large number of cultural constructs, *including* theories and conjectures. It is therefore something of a relief to be able to acknowledge that I have drawn on the most diverse sources, both ancient and modern, sometimes doing no more than harmonizing their vocabulary and making their style more lucid (and in some cases, I fear, coarsening it too). However, in view of this methodology, this work of clarification may seem less banal and insipid than one might have been tempted to think. Neutralizing a paradox may, in fact, mean many things. Generally, though, *one* of the things it means is concealing it, making it imperceptible enough to safeguard the individual and collective forms of life that have to react to the paradox existentially and *practically*, which is, logically, what matters most. Therefore, bringing this latent paradox into the full light of day may sometimes mean detaching the potential of ideas and theories from a preferential link with some specific forms of life, freeing it of its historical and ideological context, and perhaps making it available for strategies and solutions of quite another kind.

This is precisely the logic that inspires the book's confrontation with what we might call early twentieth-century German philosophical anthropology, as long as we interpret this label broadly and flexibly enough to include such varied authors as Heidegger and Schmitt, in whose works the question as to who or what we human beings are has a strategic value of the first importance.

The point that seemed to me absolutely indispensable is a feature that, with the most minor variations, recurs in the whole of this area of thought. I mean the tendency to radicalize the conceptual distinction between *world* and *environment* to the point of more or less translating it into a formula by which each animal species seems to be related to an "environment", while man, and man *alone*, is "open to the world". In the last few years, researchers in fields most influenced by molecular biology and the neurosciences have insisted on the relative implausibility of such a sharp, unequivocal distinction, and on the vaguely mythological flavour of a conception that isolates the human species from the rest of nature, attributing to it an unlikely lack of instincts, innate genetic programmes and natural bonds of any kind. Personally, I believe that such ideological distortions, while present, are ultimately insignificant, and do not substantially contaminate the underlying intuition of these anthropological conceptions. The core of this intuition, from my point of view, is precisely in the paradoxical nature of the enterprise that is here presented as a primary anthropological task: what Heidegger summarizes in the formula – as effective as it is obscure – of man as a "world-former". We shall see that "world-forming" regularly means two contrasting things: instituting a rule and celebrating the exception to it, tracing a boundary and demanding that it be crossed, reducing complexity and ensuring that complexity will erupt indefinitely. Everything suggests that this latent contradiction, which has never been fully recognized, is actually the most incisive aspect of these theories, and not a defect. On the contrary, their internal weakness is manifested precisely when the illusion of having to avoid the paradox becomes strongest. This is what happens, particularly, in the *political* sphere, in which just one of the two opposing aspirations is identified with social order, so that the other seems to be simply a threat: disorder, barbarism, crisis of presence, *and yet*, at bottom, "state of nature", inseparable from our humanity. This particular attempt to neutralize the paradox leads to the conviction of the need to "save the State", opposing any pluralist development of it, to the point of embracing the extreme reactionary consequences into which, with greater or lesser coherence, many of the main exponents of this tradition fell.

One need only add that, in point of fact, the choice of expressing the anthropological paradox only in the form of a sharp opposition between "civilization" and "state of nature" is certainly not an invention of early-twentieth-century German ideology. For centuries it had been an essential part of the complex strategy by which European culture had managed to impose the modern order on the whole of the New World. If anything, political responsibility for these theories lies in re-presenting that logic when that order had already been wrecked once and for all. Whatever the reasons, it is not for a speculative enquiry to linger over evaluating why and how seriously it had become entrenched in a conservative logic. The essential question is to try and understand what are, at the moment, the truly innovative responses, the manifestations and reactions to the paradox that have emerged in the meantime, not only in theories or in politics, but, more radically, in actual forms of life, once their emancipation from the modern canon has become clear and definitive. It is in this second line of enquiry that the book seeks to make some progress.

The complex of ideas in the book's second line of research started from an interdisciplinary investigation of dissociative phenomena that aimed to define the ongoing changes in clinical symptomatology, and to understand their causes and social implications. It started from a much-discussed view among psychiatrists and psychoanalysts that the dominant feature in many of the most widespread and typical disorders of present-day societies is the tendency to isolate and separate the potentially conflictual moments of psychic experience from each other, to the point of giving rise to what Freud had already defined a *Spaltung*, a split that vertically affects the whole of the psychic system. Unlike the classic mechanism of repression, in this case the contents of the psyche are not driven down into the unconscious, but confined to one compartment of the conscious life, rigidly separated from the rest of experience. This prevents any conflict being detonated between the Ego and the Id, but a dissociation takes shape *within* the Ego, which in a sense eradicates even the possibility of any future inter-psychic conflict.

What decided me to follow this enquiry beyond the strictly clinical dimension was the sensation – which gradually strengthened as the work progressed – that a tendency to dissociation of this kind, so far from the classical models of subjectivity, might have a decisive role not only in pathologies, but more generally in forms of life in the present, including the more "successful" ones that are generally more suitable for interacting with the present system of social communication and interaction. In this case, the ongoing change in the forms of psychic organization might be the sign of a more complex transformation, involving the institutions and the forms of collective life in equal parts. This looks more plausible if we consider that, in society too, the classical horizontal split between State and civil society has gradually given way to the network of confines and distinctions of the modern pluralist social system.

This means that what is generally described as the transition from the modern to the late modern has begun to seem a fracture that is more complex, runs deeper, and is anthropologically more significant than is usually thought. Paraphrasing Heidegger, we might say that it expresses the need to restore form to the world – that is to say, to address again the paradox inscribed in the human condition, once the conditions were gone that had allowed the modern order to restrain, conceal and put to good use the paradox at its core.

To put flesh on this hypothesis, we need to examine more closely what might seem, both psychically and socially, the most incoherent features of our ordinary experience, if we are to get a glimpse of a primary anthropological problem there. At once we find an obstacle in our path: the tendency, still dominant in research programmes, to treat the psychic and social dimensions as two independent spheres without doors or windows. This may have begun as a reaction to the hasty tendency, a century ago, of the "*Geisteswissenschaften*" to confuse the two planes, but, in the course of time, it has ended up generating theories that are so counterintuitive on the solipsism of the mind and the self-absorption of social systems, as to challenge even the most elementary good sense. I make no claims to any theory on such a delicate question, but have merely tried to keep to the general intuition that, however heterogeneous they may be, the psychic and social lives are intimately and necessarily bound up with each other, and that the particular way in which each individual culture articulates their interplay determines the light and shade of any actual historical experience. The outcome of this approach when applied to present reality is summarized in the idea that the contemporary world can usefully be described as *a world of niches*, organized into spaces halfway between the symbolic and the real – spaces that have emerged from the grey area where facts are indistinguishable from representations, and that for this very reason are suited for acting with equal intensity on psychic experience and collective communication.

From the start, I had the impression that combining the two lines of research – and thus implicitly making late-modern forms of life anthropologically exemplary – requires us to recognize, in this grey area between reality and illusion, not only the root of any psychic pathologies and social dysfunctions, but also the essential background of any decisive performance, without which our conception of human existence remains incomplete and insubstantial. Only as the work progressed did I start to be convinced that a performance of this kind might coincide with the exquisitely human capacity to transform, as part of a game, the very rules of that game. In short, it was a question of what is usually described as *creativity* – a term, incidentally, that is not wholly apt and that may risk giving the impression of an unfathomable mystery, rather than a problem accessible to real knowledge.

Whatever the truth of the matter, once this path had been chosen, I had the impression that many fragments that at first sight seemed unrelated began to form quite a coherent design. It seemed illuminating, for example, to note how psychoanalytical studies on children's play, from Winnicott on, have gradually highlighted the intimate paradox of every creative act, its inevitable rootedness in a border zone between reality and illusion, and even its affinity with pathological forms of dissociation. It seemed to me no less significant to observe that the most coherent defences of the pluralist social model rest on creativity, a striking example being Dewey's appeal for a "creative democracy".

In short, I think that behind all these attempts to consider creativity as the basic faculty of the human animal, there is a strategy to neutralize the anthropological paradox that is openly alternative to the one that has dominated modernity, and which is emerging at a theoretical level only because the actual forms of life have already been steeped in it for some time. In each case it is a question of instituting, respecting and defending a kind of niche – that is to say, a symbolic frame that sets a limit to contingency – so as to allow that limit to dissolve. Something similar, in short, to Wittgenstein's ladder at the end of the *Tractatus*, which can be thrown away as soon as one reaches the top.

An anthropological system of this kind has additional value in political theory, as Carl Schmitt made clear, if only negatively. In a passage in *The Concept of the Political* (1932), Schmitt accuses the theorists of pluralism of holding to a rudimentary and naive anthropology based on the implausible assumption of man's natural goodness and sociability, a view that could not withstand the more disenchanted and realistic intuitions of great thinkers about sovereignty, such as Hobbes or Machiavelli. Now, for as long as we restrict ourselves to the theories that have actually been put forward in the political debate, this criticism may strike home. If, on the other hand, we consider the anthropology tacitly included in social practices, then I think we must acknowledge that the forms of life that have been fashioned in a pluralist context, however partial and imperfect they may be, are an effective and coherent response to the crisis of the modern world. They may even be the *only* response that is really adequate to the difficulties that this crisis has set off.

The crucial moment in this response is the attempt to give both sides of the anthropological paradox full rights of access to the political edifice. That is to say, both the need for a limit and openness to unlimited contingency – without concealing their inner tension, but articulating it in a manifest dissociation, which is also consciously assumed as part of one's personal identity. The dark, problematic side of human nature is not repressed at all in this way, but nor is it merely expelled or frozen in the infinite conflict between civilization and state of nature. It is in this sense that we should also read the appeal to creativity, which has nothing in common with a vague, undefined niceness.

The problem is that if we consider it in this anthropologically significant sense, political pluralism no longer seems an acquisition we can take for granted, but displays all the fragility of a social experiment that is still taking its first steps. The general diversity of subjects, which increases naturally with social complexity, is one thing. The actual redefinition of the processes in which political decisions are taken is quite another. Schmitt is absolutely right when he says that a radical project of actual pluralism of this kind must face huge obstacles, must overturn the premises of the modern order (in Europe at least), and cannot actually draw any decisive advantage from the mere affirmation of democratic procedures. The fact that some of the main political subjects in the present day are claiming a model of "sovereign democracy", whose very procedures quite deliberately seek to prevent any real pluralism, is the clearest confirmation of how topical this pitiless diagnosis is, and how uncertain future global geopolitical stability.

In any case, this book can offer only a minimal contribution on such concrete questions. The real forms of a pluralist model of political decision-making are only mentioned in passing, and there is no serious attempt to examine the link between a state of emergency and the establishing of rules in present-day societies. Such questions would need to be systematically rooted in political theory, while I intend to remain throughout on the primary anthropological terrain. For similar reasons, the references to creativity are also sporadic and partial. On this question no truly searching enquiry could ignore how incisively and ambiguously linguistic creativity has re-emerged in Chomsky's work, only to be torpedoed by orthodox cognitivism and then made accessible – in part – in the blank shots, uncertainties and unsolved problems of the present-day human techno-sciences. This too would have required a different book.

For good or ill, this is a work of philosophical anthropology, and nothing else. Its essential aim is to try to understand what an idea, like Heidegger's – by which our humanity consists in our capacity to form a world – can really mean. In particular: what can constituting the human in this way really mean *today*. My main ambition has been to transfer this question, without impoverishing it too much, from the rarefied air of existential analytics to the firm ground of cultural, psychic and social experience, defined by precise spatial and temporal references. A particularly good example of a transfer of this kind, in my view, is Ernesto De Martino's analysis of the ancient Roman ritual of the *mundus*, which is dealt with at length in the penultimate chapter of the book. It seemed to me extraordinary how Heidegger's most elaborate and nebulous intuitions on the conflict between the World and the Earth were confirmed pragmatically in De Martino's study, thus becoming accessible to genuine scientific enquiry. This was all the more significant as Heidegger himself shared to the last the prejudice of academic philology, by which Roman culture had nothing to offer that was not a debased regurgitation of Greek tradition.

Though I am far from being a cultural chauvinist, I will not deny taking a certain pride in noting that it was an Italian anthropologist who refuted this prejudice – one who still awaits proper recognition in his own country as well as abroad. It may be that thought is essentially a solitary meditation, while culture is a team game, and, whether one likes it or not, one is committed to saving what is good in one's cultural tradition as soon as one starts to speak in an historical language, thus enrolling in a national culture. In the specific Italian case, the burden of the commitment is all the more essential, now that this national culture's suicidal vocation seems more determined than ever.

While the work was in progress, almost all its individual parts were discussed in seminars and conferences before an audience that had the ideal expertise for taking further or correcting the specific argument presented. I am most sincerely grateful to Laura Bazzicalupo and Enrica Lisciani, Fausto Pellecchia and Massimo Adinolfi, Igino Domanin, Fulvio Papi, Daniele Gambarara, Federico Chicchi, Marco Russo and Vincenzo Vitiello for those valuable opportunities for discussion. More than anyone else, though, I must thank Gianluigi Di Cesare, without whose help and advice my research on dissociative phenomena, which proved so decisive in the final draft, would never have seen the light of day. Elisabetta Baiocco, Marco Baleani, Francesca Borrelli, Stefano Catucci, Gino Giometti, Francesco Piro, Elettra Stimilli, Stefano Velotti, Stefano Verdicchio and Paolo Virno read early drafts of the work at various stages. Their critical comments and, in some cases, their eloquent silence showed me how to correct and rework the material into a version that I hope may seem acceptable to them all. The model of philosophical anthropology set out in the book was developed and discussed in the seminars organized by the journal *Forme di vita*. Among those taking part at these meetings, apart from those already cited, I must mention at least Francesca Piazza, Felice Cimatti and Marco Mazzeo, whose specific expertise in the philosophy of language and mind were most helpful. No less so was the contribution of Tommaso Russo Cardona, an exceptional scholar whose early death leaves a gap in the whole of our small research community.

Less directly, the ideas in the book developed in the context of the Italian debate on bio-politics and show the influence in particular of the work of Giorgio Agamben, Roberto Esposito, Pietro Montani and Paolo Virno. Even where there are no specific references, I am perfectly aware of the fact that there is not a page in the book that is not, directly or indirectly, reworking or responding to the work of one or another of these four authors.

Finally, a study that gives so much space to the anthropological value of childhood and the creativity of play could not but be influenced decisively by the constant presence of my three children. From them and their friends I discovered that dissociation may be a decisive – and dangerous – existential strategy. That is why I would like to dedicate the book to them: to Maddalena, Adrian and – last, but not least – to Emma, who for nine months was competing with my typescript as to which of the two should come into the world first. In the end, she won.

Chapter 1

Niches

> Nec certam sedem, nec propriam faciem,
> nec munus ullum peculiare tibi dedimus,
> o Adam, ut quam sedem, quam faciem
> quae munera tute optaveris, ea, pro voto,
> pro tua sententia, habeas et possideas.
> Definita caeteris natura intra praescriptas a
> nobis leges cohercetur. Tu, nullis angustiis
> cohercitus, pro tuo arbitrio, in cuius manu
> te posui, tibi illam praefinies. Medium te
> mundi posui, ut circumspiceres inde
> comodius quicquid est in mundo.[1]
>
> Giovanni Pico della Mirandola, *Oratio de hominis dignitate*

1 Ontology of the present

The question these thoughts revolve around is anything but new. On the contrary, it is almost a classic of modern culture. To adopt a piece of precise technical jargon, we might describe it as the *interpenetration* between the *mental* operations of individual psychic systems and the *communicative* process that structures social systems. Put less rigorously (but more clearly), I want to examine the link between what happens *in our heads* and what takes place in the *public* dimension – in parliaments, and in the workplace and social institutions.

What *may* prove new, however, is the empirical material I shall be using. On principle, I have chosen to concentrate essentially on *contemporary* forms of life, and shall also foreground the authentically innovative features in the psychic, social

1 "We have not given you, oh Adam, a fixed home, or your own face or a special talent, so that you might have and possess the appearance and talent you yourself would choose, according to your desires. For other beings, nature is defined and, as it were, confined within laws that we have prescribed them, while in your case, unhampered by any limitation, you yourself will trace your limits, following your judgment, in whose hands I have placed you. I have placed you in the midst of the world, so that from there you might observe more conveniently all that there is in the world."

and communicative dimensions that cannot be reduced to the classical models of modern culture. In this respect, I aim to contribute to what Michel Foucault called an "ontology of the present", offering it as a systematic attempt to answer the question "what's happening *now*?", and it goes without saying that *now* – the present – coincides in our case with that profound and problematic process that, for want of more incisive criteria, is still designated as the transition from *modern* to *late modern*. I start from the assumption that in this epochal transition many things are changing, in our heads at least as much as in the public world, but that a more subtle transition may specifically concern the *correlation* between the two dimensions of the psychological and the social, and that this change, less evident but deeper, may be the most direct cause of the disorientation so typical of this historical phase.

It would be both reductive and naive, however, to try to reflect on our contemporary situation without any more general reference to history, nature or the human condition, as if the present were a world apart that did not share the same matrix with every other age and every other culture. Against this simplification, it is worth recalling that the expression "ontology of the present" deliberately invokes an oxymoron: while, on the one hand, it obliges us to focus on what is happening *only now*, at the same time it openly declares an *ontological* intention in relation to what has *always* been part of how we have defined our *Dasein*. It is this short circuit between current events and ontology that sanctions the strictly "philosophical" character of enquiries that can be classified under this heading, which, in a field of strictly contemporary phenomena, seek to highlight in each case some primary anthropological features, mostly misunderstood or repressed in the idea of human nature that has been transmitted by modern culture.

In the specific case of *this* research, the anthropological feature in question is the typically human tendency to situate practices in a circumscribed, delimited space, isolated from the outside and closed up in itself by a symbolic boundary that makes of it *a world inside the world*, or, to use a conventional term, a *niche*. In accordance with the research programme I have just traced, this term "niche" will therefore be used systematically for both registers, that of the present world and that of ontology, so as to focus the *specific* modality in which the social and psychic planes interweave in contemporary forms of life – a modality that *distinguishes* the late-modern condition from what came before. At the same time I shall be suggesting that this modality, which is so distinctive and new, may teach us something decisive as to how human beings have *always* tended to organize their existence in closed symbolic spaces, delimited and protected from the infinite variety of the outside world. To perform this function, the term must acquire a technical meaning, which, I hope, will gradually become clearer and more solid in the course of the work. What convinced me to choose this word as the key concept, however, was the fact that, if we look closely, a similar duality of registers is already implicit, at bottom, in its current use.

The term "niche" usually suggests a defined and limited space, in clear contrast with the global extension of the great social processes. A "niche" cultural form or product is one aimed exclusively at a restricted sector of the public that shares a specific code of values or behaviours. If only by contrast, then, the concept of "niche" is related to the context of globalization, and it has meaning only with this kind of context as a premise. In the not-too-distant past, *any* cultural performance was naturally situated in the framework of a specific culture, a language, or a system of beliefs and rules shared exclusively by the members of a particular community. One might want to conclude from this that, in their way, all cultures of the past were niches, but dilating the concept so unrestrainedly would simply flatten any difference and obscure real problems. The cultural delimitations of the past were dictated by objective reasons: territorial borders, geographical distances, independent traditions and, in the broadest sense, cultural divisions that the means of communication available at the time could not eliminate technically. So, though people were well aware of the existence of any number of exotic civilizations and cultures in the distant past, we may imagine that the limited and peripheral nature of their *own* cultural world was endured – denied and contradicted, even – but never deliberately contrived with the precise intention of distinguishing themselves from all that was outside it.

Actually, as we shall see, we may be supposing too much here. For the moment, however, it will allow us to focus more precisely the concept of niche in the *first* of its current meanings. We can say that a "niche" is a symbolic boundary that survives after all the extrinsic reasons that might justify its existence have been removed; a limit, in other words, that has no substantial reason other than *the need to draw a limit* that distinguishes an inside from an outside. The question is: where does this need come from? Is it, too, marginal and contingent, or is it concealing a primary anthropological root? At once this question brings us up against the *other* semantic sense of our key term, linked to the elementary assumptions of modern biology.

It is now generally accepted that every living organism is related to a specific *ecological niche*. The term indicates much more than a spatial delimitation, like that linking fish to the sea or penguins to the snow. Strictly speaking, the niche to which each species is genetically tied consists of a limited series of biologically significant signals (the shadow of a predator, the pattern on the coat of a conspecies of the opposite sex, and so on), which, in suitable conditions, set off further innate programmes of behaviour that are essential for survival and reproducing the species. Now, an intuition on which much of twentieth-century European philosophical anthropology is based is that, as a result of a series of evolutionary processes, this clear, unequivocal correlation between signals and instinctive programmes tends to be reduced in human beings, tends to become more flexible and secondary, to the point of having only a marginal role in actual survival strategies. We are, in other words, quite exceptionally "open to the world": essentially without a genetically prescribed niche and exposed "to a sensory overload, a flood of stimuli without any precise biological meaning" (Gehlen 1940, pp. 35–36). Let us leave aside for the moment the many dubious and debatable aspects of the best-known versions of this intuition, in authors like Scheler and Gehlen, and keep to its central core, whose substance has never been refuted by the research over the last century – the distinction between the general correlation every living creature has with an environment, and the *openness to the world* that is specific to the human animal. One sees at once that this openness brings with it an essential ambivalence. On the one hand, it is the premise for our *congenital flexibility* as human beings, our capacity to adapt to any environment and, still more, to remodel any environment to our needs. On the other, unfiltered exposure to an infinite chaos of contingencies cannot fail to be perceived above all as a *threat*, which obliges us to construct a protective shell, or, in other words, an *artificial niche* in place of the congenital one.

Biologically speaking, the human condition thus seems to be situated between two basic, connected and antithetical demands: that of *openness*, which leads to exploring and experimenting any possible environment and, still more, adjusting one's form of life to the *virtual infinity* of these environments; and that of *protection*, which leads to carving out a world in the world and defining the confines of a niche that will be a clear watershed between the familiar figures inside it and the indistinct background that it excludes.

The obligation to satisfy both these antithetical forces in the same form of life creates an inevitable split, which cannot be solved by compromise or a simple balancing act between the two poles. As we shall see, the two demands are not simply in conflict, but overlap, blend and reproduce while remaining essentially opposed, until, deep down, there leaks out a *paradoxical* dynamic that is mainly repressed in current anthropological and political conceptions, which tend to favour one or other of the two sides. Here, however, we shall follow the opposite strategy, considering this basic duality, this problem or open paradox, as a feature of the human condition in general, and make it our basis for measuring the coherence of each specific, particular and contingent response to what we are defining as an *anthropological paradox.*[2]

It is logical enough to expect any attempt to balance the two aspirations to be intrinsically precarious, and exposed to a dual threat. Openness to unlimited contingency might lead to the collapse of all expectations and all lasting institutions, or, vice versa, the need for protection might impose on the world the obtuse repetitiveness of a sham environment created as a defence *against* the world. Dodging this dual threat, creating a harmonious and relatively stable equilibrium between the two wavering poles, has plausibly been a primary task in every period *both* for the public institutions *and* for the psychic operations that ensure the unity of our minds. We might reasonably suppose that it is on precisely this terrain that the two dimensions – the psychic and the social – are inevitably led to correlate, to shape themselves on each other, and to structure themselves on the same symbolic codes and references. In any case, we know that there are *many* ways of balancing

2 I should mention that the expression "anthropological paradox" has already been used by Pandolfi (1997) to indicate an internal contradiction of anthropological research, which, though guided by a critique of ethnocentrism, yet at the same time expresses a kind of latent collusion with the colonial project. Here, as we can see, the expression is used in a wholly different sense, and I do not think the use of it should give rise to any misunderstanding.

openness and protection, that different societies, cultures and forms of life can offer different solutions to the paradox, and that each solution has its reasons, its needs, its advantages and its specific dangers. It may be useful to draw comparisons on individual aspects, but any value judgement or supposed hierarchy between different periods, cultures and worlds is hardly tenable.

The book will argue that, on this terrain, contemporary society is tending towards solutions and paradigms that are *different* from those that guided classical modernity. To wonder whether this is, in the abstract, good or bad is probably a futile exercise. It is much more practical to learn to understand *where we are*, to develop concepts that are adequate to describing the new context, and to try to distinguish the internal risks and opportunities, the latent conflicts, and the various forces in play.

2 Environment and world

Summarized in a formula, our working hypothesis will be that the contemporary world can usefully be depicted as *a world of niches*, rather than, say, a world of nations and peoples, following the classical modern scheme, or a world that is basically unified, in which any kind of boundary or distinction has no meaning, as in the more superficial versions of globalization.

Naturally, in these early stages, the formula is still without any defined meaning. It is to be taken solely as a way of finding our bearings, almost as a provocation whose only objective for the moment is to bring out the latent complexity of concepts that we normally use naively and inappropriately. The first of these concepts is the term *world*, to which we usually attribute the simple meaning of an objective reality, a geographical space, which, like a great cake, is cut up differently in every age, while its sections remain equally *real*, measurable and palpable. To understand in what sense this current understanding of the term does not fit the problems we are facing, let us go back to the distinction between animal *environment* and human *world*, which we mentioned earlier.

This distinction was introduced in the first half of the twentieth century by one of the great pioneers of modern biology, Jakob von Uexküll, whose research was later a constant *point de repère* for all the attempts of European philosophy to deal constructively, and not just polemically, with the new life sciences. In the back-and-forth of this reception a mass of nuances and implicit connotations was deposited on the concepts Uexküll had introduced. This means a little patience will be necessary to unravel this tangle of meanings, but I believe it is the best way to gain an overall view of the problems that a project such as ours is bound to raise, as soon as it brings together two apparently opposing terms such as "world" and "niches".

Following Uexküll's (1934) account, then, it is an anthropocentric illusion that makes us believe that the cow and the cicada, the duck and the butterfly, to all intents and purposes cohabit in the same field and share the same portion of the world. Biological research teaches us that, actually, each of these organisms is open to a restricted and specific range of signals, which means that it is, in a certain sense, *enclosed* in a niche that does not interact with that of the other species, unless indirectly. Thus, the spider weaves its web, following an innate programme, and though its web is exactly calibrated to the weight and perceptions of a fly, its weaver, strictly speaking, *knows nothing* of the fly.

The specificity of the human animal has only a marginal presence in Uexküll's book. He does no more than mention the possibility that our "world" is not so very different from the environment of any other species: no more than the niche set aside for an animal with notable, but certainly not supernatural, adaptive capacities. As it was developed by philosophical anthropology in the following decades, this reductive hypothesis was quickly set aside in favour of a sharp conceptual distinction between animal environment and human world, which insisted instead on the open, undefined and, literally, *unheimlich* – i.e. disturbing, monstrous – character of the "world" as a specific correlate of human experience. One might well find this attempt to separate our humanity from our animality somewhat strained. However debatable this is, though, the distinction had the merit of bringing out the primary task to which every human culture seems bound: escaping the flood of contingencies, and unifying possible experience in a coherent and ordered "world".[3]

However, how is this cultural imperative to be carried out in practice? The apparently most simple answer is to suppose that cultural institutions and the customs and techniques that are handed down contribute in each culture to building a reassuring, familiar world to *oppose* the external chaos, tracing the perimeter of an *artificial niche* that compensates for the lack of a precise biological correlate. This is essentially the answer to be found in Arnold Gehlen's theory of institutions, and which, less explicitly, inspires Plessner's formula for the primary political task of every human society – that of carving out for itself "an environment from the world" (*eine Umwelt aus der Welt*: Plessner 1931, p. 107). In this formula, as we can see, the two terms *Umwelt* and *Welt* swap their usual places, and it is our species that is assigned the task of constructing for itself an environment, rather than a world, although the sense of the phrase remains unequivocally that of opposition between an ordered, familiar sphere, produced by culture, and a disordered and disturbing one, comparable to a Hobbesian state of nature.

There is nothing equivocal or mysterious in this terminological fluidity in itself. Yet, really, we should marvel that, without any particular straining, the same term

3 The prototype of this conceptual distinction between environment and world is traced by Gehlen, for whom "[t]he clearly defined, biologically precise concept of the environment is thus not applicable to man, for what 'environment' is to animals, 'the second nature', or culture, is to man; culture has its own particular problems and concept formations which cannot be explained by the concept of environment but instead are only further obscured by it" (Gehlen 1940, pp. 79–80). No one today would probably want to formulate the distinction in such clear-cut terms, but this does not mean that the problems inherent in this dichotomy human/animal have really been solved, or even fully defined.

"world" can indicate indifferently both poles of the distinction: both the unlimited contingency that is a correlate of human experience, and the symbolic order that has to deal with it. At least in the first instance, this Janus-like character of the concept of "world" is clearly a paradox, given that the symbolic order has the precise function of *denying* contingency, opposing the indefinite, the formless and the possible with a complete and coherent system of definitions, forms and laws. In the following pages, however, we shall learn to understand more clearly that this is no accidental confusion, nor a merely rhetorical expedient: rather, this semantic ambiguity reveals the intrinsically paradoxical nature of a distinction that, to be effective, will inevitably tend to dissolve of its own accord.

First, let us note at once that the symbolic order can only succeed in rejecting unlimited contingency if order manages to cover *the whole world*, and not just a part of it, and it leaves outside itself nothing but non-being, the void, nothingness. In practical terms, this means that the stability of a symbolic system depends on its capacity to include every kind of metaphysical enquiry on what is *beyond* its given confines and distinctions: beyond the heavens, beyond life, and so on. However, there is another bond, still deeper, that makes the cultural "niche" inseparable in human experience from what crosses its confines. As we have seen, the value of this niche is measured by the need to limit the absolute contingency of exposure to the world, separating what really does have meaning from everything else that can simply be dismissed as mere noise. As it is a cultural construct, and not an innate premise, the process of setting up this valuable distinction between signal and noise actually *begins from their lack of distinction*. In this way it is inevitable that indistinctness, chaos and unlimited contingency are an essential part of cultural procedures and actually contribute to defining their basic operation and creative core.

As in a Möbius strip or the more classical Hegelian *Aufhebung*, the split that establishes the "world" must first distinguish an ordered space from a formless background, so that it can then effectively cancel this distinction, transcribing the background *within* the order, which only then will have value as an order of the world as such. From Plato's *Timaeus* to Wittgenstein's *Tractatus*, metaphysics has continued to chew over this paradox, and it is its inner complexity that decrees the inadequacy of any attempt to solve unequivocally and definitively the opposition between *heimlich* and *unheimlich*: between what is familiar and what is disturbing, between the limit and the unlimited, order and chaos. Recognizing in an openness to the world the basic feature of the human condition, twentieth-century philosophy tacitly sought to make of this paradox the inevitable terrain for any future anthropological project.

To grasp what is really at stake in what might otherwise seem abstract metaphysical niceties, we should recall that in this period, especially in Germany, the idea was growing that openness to the world was not just an anthropological marker, but also defined an essential *political* task. This can be seen in what is perhaps the most incisive exposition of the problem: that provided by Heidegger in a course of lessons in 1929, structured as a long commentary on three fundamental ontological assertions: "The stone is worldless; the animal is poor in world; man is world-forming." Published posthumously in his complete works, the course is rightly regarded as a masterpiece of phenomenological analysis, revealing a complex ontology of life that starts from concrete phenomena such as profound boredom, the phototropism of insects, or the elementary structure of enunciation. Much less popular was his attempt a few years later to transpose onto the *political* plane the aspiration of "constructing a world", comparing it to the decision of a "people" to place their supposed historical destiny before any individual will or deviation and, indeed, before any *pluralism* within the social dynamic.[4]

As will readily be appreciated, it is a delicate point, which also involves the thorny question of the relation between Heidegger's philosophy and totalitarian ideologies. Dismissing this political shift, however, as a mere accident would not, I think, be a satisfactory solution – for various reasons. First of all, because mistrust for the political model of modern pluralism is not the personal idiosyncrasy of a few authors, but a trend common to a significant area of the culture of the period, of which Heidegger is only the most representative voice. Second, because the relation between *human nature* and *political institutions*, which is the real heart of the question, is not a problem that can be confined to a specific period and historical contingency, and with which contemporary culture can therefore delude itself as having settled its accounts. This is confirmed by the fact that its classical paradigm, starting from the human/animal comparison, was already set out in its main lines in Aristotle's *Politics*.

Without a clear vision of this classical background, it is impossible to grasp the deep meaning of the model of political anthropology that emerged in Europe between the two world wars and explain how this one model could inspire both totalitarian ideologies and the most radical and significant forms of critical thought. As, at bottom, the problems have changed less than might appear on the surface, without a direct comparison with this historical precedent we might easily reproduce the same ambivalence unconsciously, and so, if we want to project the social and political dynamic of the present onto a primary anthropological background, we will do well to remind ourselves of at least the main lines of the speculative context in which Aristotle presents human beings as "political animals", and try to understand what effects this classical model had on Heidegger and, more generally, on twentieth-century European culture.

4 See Heidegger (1934). This course of lessons had been originally announced under the title "The State and Science", in which the political intention was explicit. The later modification clearly reflects Heidegger's uncertainty and the difficulty of his position after resigning as rector. According to the volume's editors, it also aroused "surprise and irritation" among the Nazi functionaries who were intending to follow the course. Whatever the reason, even in the new version the idea of man as "world-forming" is at the root of a conception that sees political decision, state sovereignty and the homogeneousness of a people as inseparable. We shall return several times to this conception, of which Schmitt offers the most complete version.

3 World-formers?

As has been observed (see Agamben 1995), Aristotle makes a sharp distinction between the undifferentiated process of life, indicated by the term *zoé*, and the specific form that life acquires in each concrete case, expressed by the term *bios*. The distinction is not the equivalent of that between animal and human life because – as Aristotle insists – there are different forms of life, and so different *bioi*, not only between men, but also, by nature, between animals too. Some, in fact, "are carnivores, others herbivores, others omnivores", and their way of life is intrinsically different, as is, among human beings, that of the nomad, the peasant, the hunter or the brigand (see *Pol.* I, 1256a). In non-human animals, however, the *bios* is substantially co-extensive with the species: there is one form of life for the lion and one for the lamb, but each species has *one* and one only. The task of impressing each time a particular form on life does not fall either to the individual or the group, because, at least in its main lines, this form is already predefined in the legacy of instincts innate to the species. In short, *bios* and *zoé* are one and the same thing for them, seamlessly linked, and so *surviving* and *living* are, in this context, two equivalent concepts and, almost, synonymous. In the case of human beings, however, the plurality of *bioi* has a sense that is diametrically opposite. If the hunter's form of life, or the peasant's, or the brigand's, are all equally accessible to members of the same species, it is because *none* of them is already prefigured in the inherited patrimony of the species. Examining this anomaly, to the point of wondering whether it is possible "that the carpenter and the cobbler have certain characteristic actions and activities, and a human being has none" (*Eth. Nic.* I, 1097b), Aristotle's work provides what is in effect the first explicit treatment of what I have called the "anthropological paradox". Only in the case of the human animal, in fact, does there seem to be a fundamental *natural* gap in force between *zoé* and *bios*, so that, with no innate instincts and inhibitions to guide him towards a specific *ergon*, he is virtually *capable of anything*, which, for Aristotle, makes him, depending on context, both "the best of creatures" and "the worst of all" (*Pol.* I, 1253a).

In the classical conception, the deciding factor in this oscillation is the *political* institution, which has the task of shaping this dangerous and flexible potentiality into the mould of a shared form of life, welding together *zoé* and *bios*. This is the sense of Aristotle's formula sanctioning the natural foundation of the *polis*, which "originates in the bare needs of life, and continues in existence for the sake of a *good* life" (1252b). A good life means, in this case, impressing on life a *form* whose stability is distinct from general survival. What holds the two together is sewn with the fine thread of a patient cultural *refining* of the instincts – an operation that is always precarious and exposed to the risk of a denatured *bios* upsetting the balance. An example of this would be slavery, in which attachment to *zoé* means giving up all rights regarding the form of the *bios*. However, it is also the destiny of one like Midas, who was driven to pointlessly accumulating unlimited wealth, because he was "concerned with living and not with a good life" (1257b).

Heidegger's 1929 course does not refer directly to these passages from the *Politics*, but his ontology of the human derives entirely from reflecting on Aristotle. So he was neither misunderstanding nor simplifying when, a few years later, attempting to transpose it to a political context, he made the task of "world-forming" actually follow the need to inscribe *zoé* in *bios*, subordinating the logic of survival to that of a "good life" that ensures the identity of the Self on an individual and collective plane (see Heidegger 1934). That it is *politics* that has the primary anthropological burden is in turn dictated by this classical approach. The point is that in twentieth-century European society, political institutions changed profoundly. Above all, their context changed, and they now found themselves literally encircled by adversaries and threats of a completely new kind.

The main social systems – from economics to law, from culture to science – have become increasingly autonomous of politics, entrusting themselves more and more to the power of the market – the very kind of accumulation that is "concerned with living and not with living well", which Aristotle had described in wholly negative terms. The result has been ever more extensive control over the life of the individual, organized *not* by politics, but by economic power in itself, in the name *not* of a form of life, whatever it might be, but of an expansion of survival, a concern for improving to the utmost the process of biological reproduction, which has been chosen as the universal criterion of well-being. From a point of view like Heidegger's, a development of this kind amounts to an extreme threat: that we might be definitively expropriated of our capacity to "form a world", to be driven into unprecedented *worldlessness*, a kind of lapse into animalism, much darker and more senseless than any authentic animal life. It is against this threat that the traditional arsenal of European politics was mobilized, starting from the binomial people/State.

That, on the political plane, this move had in its time disastrous consequences is an established historical fact, but that is not necessarily sufficient to dismiss as a false alarm the *threat* Heidegger indicated. It was, in any case, a threat that was immediately taken up in the post-war period by all the most radical critics of the modern political system: from Kojève to Arendt, from Anders to Foucault. It may be, in short, that the crisis of the modern model is really so profound as to threaten *the anthropological root of politics*, and there is no way of dissolving this doubt apart from becoming clear about the series of phenomena that Heidegger summarizes in the formula – as incisive as it is cryptic – of "world-forming" man.

Meanwhile, it was precisely the problematic combination of psychic and social planes, which is the subject of our enquiry, that made this formula incorrigibly opaque. As early as the conclusions to his 1929 course, Heidegger had been careful to insist that it was not the individual "running around in the street" (Heidegger 1930, p. 531) that was "world-forming", but man *as such*, or "the *Dasein* in man". The problem, however, is to understand how general, anonymous belonging to *Dasein* can in practice affect modalities of individual existence to the extent of impressing a specific form on life, related to *particular* experience of the world. In Heidegger the answer to this question began to take a precise direction in his course of 1934, which openly took as its theme the "political" significance of the question, and this, as we shall see, was no accident.

His answer hinges on his identification of *language* as the essential dimension for the construction of the world. In this case too, it is the dichotomy human/animal that indicates the way: while every living species finds the "circle" of its environment traced in a series of instinctive *signals*, the open order of the "world" germinates in the profound unity of meanings and linguistic categories. Now, language acquisition in itself is by definition a universal and necessary anthropological feature. If the world is formed in language, then, it confirms that this construction overrides individual contingency and relates to "man *as such*" in his general quality of a speaking animal. On the other hand, the German *Sprache*, as is generally known, indicates both *language* in general and the historically developed *language* of a particular community: German, French and so on. The world that takes on form in language will therefore be, in each case, the correlate of a particular community, inseparable from the "historical *Dasein* of a people" and the national State, which is the direct manifestation of this *Dasein*.[5]

Actually, this open appeal to the identity of a people and its political institutions was to remain a brief parenthesis in Heidegger. In his later writings, as early as the essay on art of 1936, his attention shifted gradually towards other ways of "opening a world", starting from artistic creation. To effect this diversion, he had only to place the limited sense of *Sprache* – as historical *language* – in the background in favour of its extended meaning, and this linked openness to the world with the faculty of *language* in general. It is reasonable to suppose that this shift of emphasis was determined, at least in part, by historical circumstances, but even on the strictly speculative plane, the logical connection between language, people and State was, from the start, somewhat uncertain. In effect, the insistence on the importance of language in constructing a collective identity was a prerogative of nineteenth-century *European* nationalism, at least in part as a reaction to the "Creole" nationalism of the American and Asian colonies, which obviously did not give similar weight to the supposed national language, which was either non-existent or derived from the colonizers (see Anderson 1991). In the European context itself, on the other hand, the coupling of language and national identity, more than a fact, was an ideological construct, designed to cancel the innumerable differences between regions, dialects, ethnic groups and cultures that were often pretty heterogeneous. It was a unification that was rarely without violence, in which complex social operations – like the institution of bureaucratic systems, schools, armies and frontiers – were clearly decisive and only minimally ascribable to language, and were in any case transmitted by a *written* language that was parallel to and distinct from that of everyday experience.[6] The reconstruction of

5 See Heidegger (1934, pp. 165–169).

6 As well as the classic studies by Hobsbawm (1990) and Anderson (1991), see also De Mauro (1963), who claims (p. 41) that hardly 2.5% of the population habitually communicated in the national language at the time of Italian unification.

these social processes is an important chapter in contemporary history, which we can only glance at here. For the development of my argument now it is essential only to recognize in *all* these social operations a hybrid of accidental selection, political planning, and pure and simple *pretence* on the part of the media – a mixture that was to become explosive in the global society of the present, when it is now clear that the correlate of every "imagined community" *is not a world, but a niche*, artificially carved out of the context of a social dynamic that is of planetary dimensions.

Heidegger's *Weltbildung* has no trace of this turbid evolutionary combination, either in the "political" version of 1934 or in the more speculative ones of the following years. There is, however, one feature of this internal development that deserves particular attention. Unlike Gehlen, Heidegger was clear from the start that if it was to be something more than an artificial niche, the human world had to include *within it* an openness to unlimited contingency, and not just drive it out into exile. There was no room for this thought, however, in the political outline of 1934, though we can see it reappear in the later writings, in contexts that were deliberately extraneous to a theory of the institutions in the strict sense. In this connection, the most famous formula is the one linking the institution of the world to the emergence of the *earth*, understood as primal opacity and indistinctiveness: "World is grounded on earth, and earth rises up through world (…) In its resting upon earth, the world strives to surmount it. As the self-opening it will tolerate nothing closed. As the sheltering and concealing, however, earth tends always to draw the world into itself and keep it there" (Heidegger 1936, p. 26).

It is all too easy to lament the abstract and vaguely mythological character of this dialectic between world and earth, opening and closure. Yet, in it is expressed again the *political* intent to oppose the worldlessness and rootlessness imposed by modernization, but without falling back on a purely conservative defence of cultural traditions threatened by progress. The attempt, in other words, was that of balancing and uniting the demand of openness with that of protection, so as to make Aristotle's problem of the "good life" current once again. However, the traditional distinctions between *bios* and *zoé*, human and animal, world and environment, now seem inadequate to transmit this perspective, precisely because they are impotent in the face of the intrinsically paradoxical nature of the task of "world-forming", considered in its existential sense. The task was all the more difficult, thanks to the mistrust that Heidegger still harboured for "inauthentic" forms of individual existence – that is to say, the accidental and subjective *psychic* processes of "the human being running around in the street". This mistrust betrays a recurrent feature of modern German culture, from Hegel down to Luhmann: the tendency to recognize a value in psychic experience only insofar as it reflects the social dynamic, rejecting it as the empty background noise of history when it fails to do that. Justified or not, this *anti-psychology* helps keep theoretical thought suspended in a limbo where any actual hold on the combination of the psychic and social planes is prohibited. Not only is the sphere of the political institutions now out of bounds, but there is something irretrievably obscure in the link between the *third person*, which expresses "man's *Dasein*", and the *first person* of each individual subject, committed to his own self-constitution, harried by an ocean of imponderable contingencies, and therefore forced to select, and to trace the uncertain and precarious perimeter of the horizon of his own life.[7]

It is from here that we shall try to start, from the next chapter on. Specifically, we shall try to patiently reconstruct this story in *realistic* terms, without removing from it the fortuitous and arbitrary aspects that make it inaccessible to any abstract apologia of the "political community". It is this very realism that imposes from the outset a slight but substantial modification of Heidegger's formula. Let us say: human beings, at least those in the present, are essentially *niche-forming*. The confines we fix separate each time a segment of experience from a network of external contingencies *with which we must inevitably coexist*, and which we cannot dismiss as non-existent, but which cannot be fully included in the horizons of our life without our inner world going up in flames. This requires boundaries to be set, boundaries that are ephemeral and intimately paradoxical, and which can only remain standing with a component of *illusion*, and, hence, by systematic recourse to psychic mechanisms that European modernity had usually expelled from the confines of rationality. It is on this terrain, turbid but practical, that we must work at tracing the subtle tension between openness and closure, between the need to protect oneself and the need to expose oneself to unlimited contingency, which is the background to any form of effective life.

Whether these practices can, in the not-too-distant future, point towards the possibility of a "good life" is still doubtful. One can at least hope, in the meantime, that investigating them opens up a more transparent and responsible theoretical perspective than that which, in its time, led European philosophy to flirt with totalitarian ideologies.

4 The vertical split

These preliminary reflections could generate a misunderstanding that it would be well to dissolve at once. They might give the impression that the link between the psychic and the social planes has remained an essentially marginal issue in modern culture, if not one that has been completely ignored. On the contrary, if I presented our topic as "classical" at the outset, it was because the dominant outlook of our culture has given a decisive role to the conviction that psychic and social dynamics – or, to put it in "modern" terms, *subjective* and *objective* rationality – were two faces of the same coin: the moments, the expressions and the articulations of a single process.

In Hegel, in particular, this unity was also formally sanctioned by the use, for both poles, of the same keyword: the *Geist*, which is interpreted as a "subjective" and "objective" *Geist*. Even in authors who are more cautious in the words they

7 On this problem, see Esposito (2006).

use, there prevails an idea that in both dimensions everything revolves around the same operation of *unifying multiplicity*. In short, the Ego has the task of subjecting the primal partial and polymorphic drives to the unity of a moral conscience that can desire and act *on the basis of laws*, and so is compatible with the requirements of civilized life; and, in wholly similar terms, the State is assigned the function of subjecting to the civil law the centrifugal drives of the *multitude*, thus establishing the unity of a *people*.

Of course, what I have just traced is only an abstract scheme, which takes not the slightest account of the wealth and variety of the theories that germinated in the golden centuries of European modernity. This type of elementary schematism should allow us, however, to concentrate on two features that, in my view, constitute the real cornerstones of the modern paradigm: on the one hand, the idea of a *hierarchical* relation of subordination and conflict between the symbolic plane and that of the drives; and on the other, the psychic and social dimensions hinging on the primacy of the *law*.

To grasp the profound connection between these two aspects, we should first of all note that in both of them there is a sharp break with the classical model as expounded in exemplary fashion in the *Nicomachean Ethics*. In effect, although the Greeks may have expressed more clearly than anyone else the tension between the plane of the drives and the symbolic one of the *logos*, their anthropological ideal still remained that of a *synthesis*, and not a conflict, between the two psychic dimensions – a synthesis that was to be reached by a slow, gradual process of refining and practice. When achieved, however, this synthesis is expressed in a practical intelligence (*phronesis*) focused on the particular, on what is contingent and unrepeatable and which therefore *escapes* the dictates of general laws. By contrast, on the threshold of modernity the badge of human rationality became the *form of the law* itself and, at the same time, any hypothetical synthesis between intellect and drives gave way, leaving on the field only the possibility of conflict and submission.

We should note that this shift of emphasis is above all a response to the need to ensure for humanity its *exceptional* position in the cosmos. According to the new framework of the sciences, there is no natural phenomenon that does not *obey* a law. Only of ourselves, however, are we allowed to suppose that we *follow* a rule, because the law in this case is *formulated* linguistically and is thus exposed to the possibility of being negated. In short, strictly speaking, a law can be obeyed *only by those who can transgress it*: this is the new anthropological ideal of *freedom*, understood, literally, as *autonomy*, the conferring of the law on ourselves, and therefore as "independence from everything empirical and hence from nature generally" (Kant 1787, A174). As it includes the possibility of transgression, this ideal is internally related to the guarantee of an external authority: and as it is first of all autonomy from any constraint or natural automatism, it imposes the repression of any instinctive inclination.[8]

8 In Kant the logical connection between the various moments of the modern is utterly transparent. Independence from nature must be radical, and sanctioned by an

Although there were many, authoritative dissenting voices between the seventeenth and twentieth centuries, at least as regards these two basic features of the scheme, we are not straining the point to suppose that throughout these centuries their dominant position in the project and in modern ideology never really weakened. We find it already clearly expressed in Hobbes and it can still be glimpsed in some crucial passages of the twentieth century that would otherwise have had little in common, such as Freud's theory of "civilization and its discontents" and Carl Schmitt's doctrine of the State.[9] It was only around the mid-century, after the drastic hiatus of the two world wars, that the scheme inexorably came under strain, both in the ambit of emerging *theories* and in the capacity to find confirmation in the *facts*.

On the theoretical plane, the crisis was very probably set off by the profound transformation that gradually affected the biological sciences, neurosciences and cognitive psychology in the second half of the twentieth century, and, in part, the social sciences through systems theory. The main vector of this evolutionary leap was the systematic adoption in what were once the "*Geiteswissenschaften*" of methods, tools and experimental techniques borrowed from the natural sciences. The result was the genesis in a few decades of what may rightly be called the new *human techno-sciences*, programmatically directed to the possibility of manipulating and technically reproducing the constituent processes of the human, from the biological level to that of intelligence and symbolic communication.

Investigating the implications and repercussions of this change in knowledge, which is still in progress, would take us far from our path.[10] We may easily guess, however, that the exceptional status reserved for humanity in the modern paradigm, and the metaphysical premise of our virtual "independence from nature generally" cannot readily be reconciled with the new lines of research. In any case, far more than the underlying theoretical options, what has contributed to obscuring the connection between the psychological and the social planes has been the *style* of the new experimental forms of knowledge, in which extraordinary progress in the precision of measurements and the rigour of research programmes has been accompanied so far by a striking drop of interest in the great speculative framework. Although it has not been particularly ostentatious, this shift in scientific attention from the big picture to the detail has an immediate spin-off for our own subject. Let us consider, for example, the grand analogy in which Hobbes presents the sovereign States as *magni homines* animated by the same appetites as individuals, an image so immediately effective as to have appeared on the title page of

ontological principle, if human freedom is not to be the equivalent of that of a roasting spit that, once set off, proceeds in seeming autonomy; and the civil law, if it is to be worthy of such a complete lack of natural inhibitions, must be conceived as if it were directed to a "community of devils", capable of any transgression.

9 On the subtle but profound accord between Freud's perspective and Schmitt's, see Virno (2005).

10 For a systematic consideration of the human techno-sciences, see De Carolis (2004), to which every mention in the text of the question of technique tacitly refers.

the book, which depicts the Leviathan as an anthropomorphic giant, formed by the union of the members of his subjects. Now, when the focus of research shifts onto ever more circumscribed empirical questions, such as the role of mesolimbic dopamine in psycho-dependence, or that of opinion polls in the stability of a mass democracy, analogy is inevitably demoted to mere metaphor with a purely ornamental value. It may well be true that in both fields the stability of a complex system is in question, but a highly technical research project focusing on details is too aware of the unfathomable *diversity* of the psychic and social mechanisms to give any credit to external analogies. The result is that the split between the psychic field and the social fields tends to become sharper and sharper, the more advanced and rigorous are the research programmes. In a sociological model like Niklas Luhmann's, for example, social systems prove to be endowed with a reproductive capacity and a logic all their own, compared with which, the fact that their reproduction is still entrusted to the words and actions of human beings, who are the custodians of a particular psychology, seems a marginal, if not wholly irrelevant detail. Similarly, on the opposite front, the cognitive psychology of authors like Jerry Fodor presents the "mind" as a complex, solitary machine, on whose basic mechanisms any interaction with *other* minds in that complex to-and-fro that is social communication has, in practice, not the slightest effect.[11]

This is essentially the state of our knowledge, as things stand. That the split has imposed itself *in practice* does not mean, however, that it appears as an explicit theory supported by general, enthusiastic conviction. On the contrary, for at least a decade there has been a growing tendency to recognize more or less clearly the *limitations* of this outlook, to the point of restoring full legitimacy to the classical formulas and themes of the social sciences that had been obscured for nearly a hundred years, such as the "social mind" or "collective representations". It is not easy to establish with certainty the causes of this inversion of tendency, but everything suggests that, more than the internal development of theories, it has been the objective transformation of the *facts* on which those theories were based that imposed it.

It is unquestionable that in the last few decades profound changes in collective forms of life have been surging forward at a particularly rapid pace. The most significant of these changes, however, seem to contradict entirely the split that was established in the theories, effectively putting the link between the psychic and social planes back on the agenda. In politics, for example, *identity* conflicts have taken on a new lease of life, and these are inseparable from those profound psychic factors that today make voluntary suicide a political weapon, and collective insecurity a basic factor of consensus. In the meantime, *Homo oeconomicus*, determined only

11 For a complete picture of Luhmann's conception on this point, which I have referred to in very simplified terms, see in particular chapter 6 of Luhmann (1984), which deals specifically with interpenetration. By contrast, Fodor (1981) expounds in no uncertain terms the autarkic conception of the individual mind, which is effectively shared by all the most traditional cognitive psychologists.

by rational interests, seems today a less and less convincing theoretical construct, if not wholly obsolete, in an economy dominated by the *subjective* perception of risk, trust or happiness. Finally, on the other side, the significant changes in the most widespread psychic pathologies, of which we shall see a few examples in the next chapter, bear witness to how social systems have penetrated the profound strata of the psyche, which seems incompatible with the closed, "solipsistic" vision of the individual mind defended by the most orthodox cognitive scientists.

However much these phenomena put back on the agenda the link between what would once have been described as "objective" and "subjective" *Geist*, it is clear that a mere return to the classical paradigm is ruled out on principle. Meanwhile, as we have seen, what is emerging is not a single, grand analogy between the two dimensions, but a fine-grained interpenetration that is taking shape in what is most specific and *heterogeneous* in the psychic mechanisms, and therefore most loath to allow itself to be pigeonholed in some general theory. Above all, though, what makes it impossible to return to the classical scheme is a *structural* mutation that is accompanying, deep down, the changes listed so far, and which requires a more detailed presentation, as it defines the main context of the enquiries in the following chapters.

The whole architecture of the classical scheme, as we have seen, revolved around a *horizontal split* that sharply divided above from below: the One against the many, the Ego against the forces of partial drives, the State against the conflictual pressures inside the social body. The unity of both psychic subjects and the social community was transferred to this boundary line, which made it logical for the mechanisms of both spheres to mobilize themselves in unison in its defence. Now, our conjecture here is that in the contemporary world *this horizontal caesura tends to be replaced by a network of vertical splits* that isolate and separate numerous circumscribed spaces – pseudo-environments, micro-worlds and niches – scattered at random and tending to conduct a parallel existence, to the point of ignoring or making each other intransitive, rather than entering into open conflict.

This tendential transition from one order to another has been widely noted and discussed in the last few decades, in both the psychological and social dimensions. In particular, the concept of "vertical split" has been developed by Goldberg (1999), on the basis of some suggestions by Heinz Kohut, as a key to our psychoanalytical understanding of dissociative disorders; more generally, we shall see in the next chapter that many of the most interesting contributions of contemporary psychoanalysis from very different schools and traditions agree in recognizing the mechanisms of splitting, which are usually undervalued by the classical tradition, as having decisive importance in constituting psychic identity, although their prototype is still the concept of *Spaltung*, or "Ego-splitting", which Freud himself advanced in some of his late works. At the same time, in the political field, the idea that the relentless pluralism of advanced societies might induce an incurable crisis of state sovereignty has been, if not the only, then at least one of the crucial questions in twentieth-century debate, and the sequence of writings by Carl Schmitt, before and after the catastrophic watershed of the war, are probably the most significant document of this development. Despite all this, however, insufficient attention seems to have been paid to *correlating* the two processes. This, I would say, is no small lacuna.

Even if we want to distance ourselves as far as possible from the modern theoretical paradigm, we must inevitably acknowledge that the two elements – psychic identity and social community – are interdependent or, at least, that they have been in the *actual* history of modern society, and not only in theoretical descriptions of it. The crisis and the *parallel* transformation of both mechanisms is unlikely to be mere coincidence. Above all, it is logical to suppose that it will trigger *different* kinds of mutual correlation, whose basic features and possible lines of development we urgently need to start trying to interpret, as what is at stake in this development is no less than the concept of *civilization* that our culture has followed so far.

We should not forget, in fact, that the dual subjection – of the drives to the Ego, and of the multitude to the law – had a general anthropological value in the modern scheme, as a necessary access key to *civilized* life. It was beyond doubt that civilization involved a *cost*, that its laws imposed severe limits on the desires and freedoms of individuals, opening the way to possible pathologies on both the psychic and social planes. However, it was also taken for granted that any disintegration of civil order would impose a price that was enormously higher, if it allowed what lay in the black depths of human nature to re-emerge: its congenital lack of constraints and inhibitions on the instincts, which make human beings capable of savagery; the extraordinary *flexibility* of its openness to the world, whose paradoxical consequence is that, beyond the perimeter set by a cultural tradition, human life is unable to organize itself in a stable, lasting form.

One has every right to mistrust a conception of civilization so evidently based on the one example of Western modernity. Nevertheless, every serious attempt to reflect on our present situation has so far remained in the shadow of this classic description of the process of civilization. Consequently, the more reality departs from the model, the more this discrepancy lends itself to two diametrically opposed readings. One may foresee the advent of a substantially new model of civilization, but one with incurably vague outlines; or one may insist on the disorder, the risks and the barbarity that inevitably follow the breakdown of civilized order. Very probably, both perspectives have something to be said for them, given that, realistically, a profound transformation in the forms of life could only lead to a new equilibrium after a long transitional period, studded with malfunctions and threats whose peril it would be naive to underestimate. In short, more than a theoretical choice, the wavering traces a *real* alternative, which seems in some respects to be a reworking of the old dichotomy "socialism or barbarity", under whose banner, years ago, the first analyses of the "post-modern" world took shape in Europe, before the term degenerated into a cut-price label for every defence of the ephemeral.

We shall, of course, abstain completely from value judgements, emotional warnings or gratuitous forecasts about the future in the following pages. The current situation is so undefined and shifting that even one step forward in understanding "what is happening now" is far too ambitious. It would not, however, be an insignificant result if, in the course of time, this kind of reflection contributed to re-awakening that critical thinking whose crisis in the last few decades has impoverished the theoretical debate in Europe, making it decidedly less engrossing than in the past.

Chapter 2

Psychopathology of present-day life

> Draw a distinction.
>
> George Spencer-Brown, *Laws of Form*

1 Psychic identity and social dynamics

Let us quickly summarize the various points that have emerged so far, with a view to defining a coherent project for exploring forms of life in the present.

We might start from the forms of *vertical splitting* that seem to have been conditioning our mental and social structures more and more emphatically in recent years. They have challenged the model of order in both, a model that had dominated classical modernity. If we bring an open mind to this parallelism, I suggest we shall see more than a superficial analogy, but something that gives direct access to the most profound and significant ways in which the psychic and social mechanisms interpenetrate. This should at least lay the premises for abandoning the unilateral, mutually closed vision of cognitive conceptions of the mind on the one hand, and a sociology based on systemic models on the other.

So as not to proceed completely at random, in the previous chapter I provided a (for the moment, wholly abstract) outline of the particular configuration in which we may imagine the psychic and social processes are forced to correlate and weld with each other, and called it the *anthropological paradox*. This phrase seeks to concentrate in a single concept the complex dynamic by which *environment* and *world* are simultaneously opposed to and inscribed in each other in the human animal: the demand for both protection and openness, the need to mark out a niche and at the same time deal with unlimited contingency. If we are on the right track, we may expect contemporary manifestations of vertical splitting to bear the traces of this paradoxical dynamic, both in the psyche and in society, and that both, as a result, will feel the need to establish a reciprocal correlation. If this is so, then we are dealing with a kind of primary phenomenon inherent in our constitution, similar to those once discussed by philosophical anthropology and existential analytics. In this case, though, we have the advantage of being able to remain on the empirical terrain of the forms of psychic and social life that are actually available in the present, without having to appeal to an original, authentic dimension of dubious ontological status and, by definition, inaccessible to objective verification.

Now, as I have already recalled, the concept of a *vertical split*, which I intend to apply to both the psychic and social dimensions, is taken directly from psychoanalysis. It seems logical, then, to start our exploration from cases and problems that are intrinsic to the constitution of *psychic* identity. We can then decide whether we should extend our perspective beyond the confines of the individual mind.

In his study of this topic, Goldberg (1999) groups the variegated phenomenology of the vertical split under four main headings – circumscribed dissociation, narcissistic behavioural and personality disorders, and multiple personalities – to which we should add the area of sexual perversions, or *paraphilias*, which he deals with in an earlier study. As can be seen, it is a vast, complex field of more or less acute pathologies, many of which are now commonly recognized as syndromes typical of present-day advanced societies. These range from eating disorders to various forms of psychological dependence, from uncertainty over gender identity to pathological sexual infidelity, from criminal tendencies to the broad range of what are called borderline disorders. The idea that this variegated psychopathology of the contemporary world are simply multiple variations of what is one deep underlying structure is already interesting in itself. More than that, it is the indispensable premise for correlating the emergence of these psychic forms with a possible change in *forms of life*, whose implications it would be logical to seek in the institutional and political forms. In any case, such a bold conjecture should not be the product of abstract speculative fantasy, but emerge gradually from direct consideration of empirical examples, once we have decided on where best to start and how best to proceed.

Meanwhile, we should note that one of Goldberg's four headings is treated only marginally in his essay, despite its being, in America at least, the centre of a very lively debate at that time, though its media impact may have been out of proportion to its scientific credentials. I refer to what, until recently, was called *multiple personality syndrome*, and, in the most recent edition of the *DSM*, has been reclassified as *dissociative identity disorder* (DID). Subjects with this condition may have a certain number of distinct personalities coexisting, each with its own character, age, voice and, not infrequently, even a different name. In other words – according to the standard accounts, which have been available for years now beyond the confines of the specialist literature – a "multiple" can move abruptly from one personality to another during a conversation, changing manner and character. Thus, a thirty-year-old woman suddenly becomes a frightened child, who, just as suddenly, can give way to an aggressive adult male, and so on.[1]

1 The most famous clinical case is certainly that of "Sybil" (see Schreiber 1973), a patient of Cornelia Wilbur, whose real name was Shirley Mason. Her story has been told in many books, films and TV documentaries, which have contributed significantly to fixing the paradigm of the "multiple" in the collective imagination.

At first sight, the reason Goldberg pays little attention to this extreme case of vertical split seems to be simply the scarcity of clinical material available (Goldberg 1999, p. 13). However, it is also clear from his work that there is still serious debate over just how widespread the disorder is, and even whether it actually exists. While some of the therapists most involved are quite sure there is a "hidden epidemic" (see Steinberg and Schnall 2001, p. xvii), institutional psychiatry remains generally cool on the subject, its mistrust being directly proportional to the curiosity that such a striking and dramatic condition has inevitably aroused in popular culture. There are good reasons for this caution, not least the fact that cases of multiple personality tend to have anomalous peaks and troughs in time and space, almost like a psychiatric Halley's Comet: the syndrome spreads like an epidemic for a number of years in a specific area, and then disappears without trace for decades. There was a real explosion of cases of dissociation, for example, in late nineteenth-century Europe, just when Pierre Janet was defining his concept of hysteria, in which dissociation of identity was decisive in explaining the symptoms. The comet seems to have reappeared a hundred years later in America, where the number of cases diagnosed in the 1980s and 1990s multiplied, though with a strikingly irregular distribution. Clearly, these anomalies suggest a direct link between the spread of the pathology and some particular network of contingencies in society and communications, and it is this strong impression of a social construct, influenced by preconceived trends and expectations, that explains the reservations of specialists. Now, inverting this line of thought, the same arguments make this particular condition an ideal starting point for an enquiry such as ours, which is interested in studying precisely the connections between the psychic and the social planes – as long as we respect two methodological strategies.

In the first place, we should bear in mind the misgivings of the more cautious researchers, if we are not to be confused by episodes in which the social values of the phenomenon come into play all too directly, to the point of caricature. In effect, like any speculative problem, the question of the relation between the psychic and the social plane also has many overlapping strata, and, in the specific case of dissociative disorders, the phenomenon of multiple personality may be the most colourful stratum, but is probably the most superficial too. Actually, as we shall see, the most significant effect of the controversies that have arisen around cases of split personality has been to encourage studies and research on the concept of *dissociation* that otherwise seemed destined to be shelved as a useless legacy of nineteenth-century psychiatry. However, seeking to discover the whole of its pre-history, and finding its traces in authors, explanatory models and clinical cases that had been classified in the past under other labels, has brought to light a kind of parallel history in the interstices of psychiatric and psychoanalytic tradition. In this literature, many, if not all, of the features of the psyche that escape the classical modern conception of subjectivity congregate around a kind of fundamental operation that is presented as a way of *cutting, isolating, marking out and splitting a single segment of psychic experience as a whole*. In short, the concept of *primary dissociation* or *split* came to seem in the end the possible cornerstone of a complete re-reading of the organization of the human mind, and there is no doubt that this structural dimension of dissociation is the most significant one, even for an enquiry such as this. In short, a discussion on multiple personality may be a good starting point, but it will be essential to gain access to these deeper and more general aspects of the problem.

Second, we should note that, in recent years, the social construction of empirical reality has become, especially in the philosophy of science, a basic question in research and theoretical discussion. An example as striking as dissociative syndrome could not pass unnoticed. In fact, multiple personality has become a battleground for rival conceptions and ideologies, not only regarding the structure of the mind, the mechanism of trauma, or the actual continuity of memory, but more generally as to the existence of objective reality and the possibility of scientific knowledge that is certain and neutral. Many of these studies, which combine empirical research and speculative analysis, are of great theoretical interest and constitute an indispensable premise for any consideration of the problem. In general, however, the epistemological problems that are discussed in them are both too large and too marginal for our project, and we had best consider them only within the limits in which they actually help to delineate the connection between the psychic and the social dimension.

2 Multiple personality

Let us start, then, from the generally shared view that the subjects who display a very visible dissociative disorder almost always have a history of childhood abuse and violence. It seems logical to deduce that the split in identity begins as a defence mechanism to limit and cushion the consequences of a trauma. This hypothesis is also confirmed by the glaring analogies between dissociative syndrome in the strict sense and disorders induced in normal subjects as a result of particularly traumatic incidents such as a bomb or terrorist attack. Anyone with any knowledge of the history of psychoanalysis will recall at this point that Freud saw child abuse as having a primary etiological role in his early studies of hysteria, which were still offshoots of Janet's and Brauer's concept of dissociation. It was only later that he became convinced that fantasies and repressed sexual desires had more influence in the genesis of hysteria than any *actual* episodes of seduction and abuse.[2] This turnabout, which is at the basis of Freud's theory of repression in its canonical

2 The most explicit document on this change of direction, which also throws some light on the personal and biographical implications of the matter, is a letter written by Freud to Wilhelm Fliess on 21 September 1897. His approach up to that point, by contrast, is clearly set out in Freud (1896), where he claims that the ultimate cause of hysteria is always an adult's seduction of a child. In a note added to the text in 1924, Freud explained his change of perspective, declaring that he had not yet freed himself of the tendency to overvalue reality and undervalue fantasy (p. 345). As we shall see, the theoreticians of multiple personality follow the same path but in the opposite direction, shifting the emphasis from infant fantasies to reality.

form, has often been contested in recent years, sometimes fiercely, as a form of tacit complicity with the rampant violence within the family. Given these premises, it was inevitable that the sudden explosion of dissociative symptoms rekindled these controversies, creating a barrier of mutual hostility between Freudians – flanked on this occasion by institutional psychiatry – and what in the meantime had been taking shape as a strongly ideological movement that brought together patients and therapists specializing in dissociative phenomena.

From the "objective" point of view dear to traditional clinical research, this social and ideological aspect should obviously be left on one side as alien to the pathology in itself, or, at most, registered as a distorting factor. However, the unresolved complexity of the controversy over cases of multiple personality depends largely on the fact that such a sharp distinction between the pathology in itself and the social framework that surrounds it, is impossible in practice. The most sceptical researchers have ascertained that in a decidedly high number of cases the most evident symptoms of split personality have emerged only through the stimulation, direct or indirect, of the surrounding environment, or, more simply, of a therapist close to the "movement" (see Spanos 1996, Humphrey and Dennett 1998). However, it would be naive and hasty to conclude from this that the disorder is merely *induced* by the environment. For patients of this kind, their ambivalent desire to see their fragmentation recognized and, at the same time, to acquire a firmer identity is clearly spontaneous and is even the mainspring of any future progress in the therapy. This makes it understandable that the most enthusiastic therapists tend to encourage this desire, even at the cost of abandoning the distance usually prescribed by their professional code of conduct, setting up a more direct human contact and a more or less explicit solidarity with one or another of the personalities that seem to take the stage alternately.

This kind of collusion between patient and therapist, which makes both of them the two inseparable faces of a *single* real phenomenon, is certainly not new in the history of psychiatry. Its presence is documented, for example, in the relation between nineteenth-century clinical treatment and the theatricality of the symptoms of the "great hysteria", with which the phenomenon of multiple personality shares quite a few features. What *is* new in this case is the fact that the social correlate of the disorder is not a medical institution in the strict sense, but a kind of "movement", where science mixes with ideology, publicity and general social aspects, and which inevitably tends to seek visibility and status like any other organized social subject in the present day.

The central claim of this movement is that there is a linear, direct, causal chain between the abuse suffered and repressed, the dissociation of identity, and the retrieving of the traumatic memories during therapy, leading to remission of the dissociative symptoms. In short, though they are fiercely critical of traditional psychoanalysis, the champions of multiple personality actually draw on a therapeutic model that follows Freud's first intuitions on hysteria – with an important qualification, though. What must be brought back to consciousness in this case is a *real* memory that has been rejected, not through shame or castration anxiety, but because of its traumatic violence and its incompatibility with the reassuring image of a "normal" family. The insistence on the reality of the memory clearly involves a strong element of social exposure, with the implicit reading of intra-family relations in terms of a sharp dichotomy between dominators and victims, and it is here that the main ideological-political aspect of the movement takes shape. It is a movement that, surprisingly, brings together remnants of feminism, with its denunciation of patriarchal power, and religious extremists, for whom paedophilia and incest have always been the emblems of a corrupt society.

Obviously, each new case that reproduces the dyad dissociation/abuse reinforces the movement's credibility, the social pressure it can exert, and its media visibility. Identifying and exhibiting the greatest possible number of cases is, in short, not so much a primary objective as a vital interest. Embarrassingly, though unsurprisingly, in this activity scientific research sometimes adds its voice to those of religious proselytism or company marketing, who are willing to see the message propagated by its more picturesque aspects: the esoteric aura of dissociation, hypnotic trances, or the somnambulism of the *condition seconde*. In any case, consciously or unconsciously, its effectiveness or otherwise revolves essentially around the figure of the *victim*. Recognizing oneself as "multiple" means defining oneself as a victim, thus adding one's voice to the cry of protest that the movement represents, and receiving in response – at once – a recognized identity, a symbolic compensation, and a new community to which one can belong. By the end of the 1980s the circularity of the mechanism was already clear from the fact that many of the psychotherapists close to the movement consisted of ex-patients who were now involved in identifying and helping other victims.[3]

Underlining the incidence of these social factors, however, does not mean downplaying the cognitive value of the intuitions from which the movement started. That dissociation is essentially a defence mechanism and that its pathological degeneration is mainly linked to serious childhood traumas are convictions shared by all the authors, Freud included. Conversely, even the most orthodox Freudian today will admit that the pathogenic value of child abuse was underestimated, to say the least, in the genesis of psychoanalysis. If I insist on ideological aspects that might seem marginal, my immediate motive is simply to bring out two points of general significance that we shall later see reappearing in aspects of the present-day world far removed from the clinical dimension. First, the correlation between a specific psychic condition and a specific social network seems in these examples to be an inherent structural feature that is not just linking two isolatable phenomena that already exist on their own account, but literally *gives form* to two polarities of a single figure that is inconceivable without the interpenetration of the two poles. Second, the dissociative mechanisms in this interpenetration are not being repressed or *excluded* from the social dynamic, but are highly *functional* to the development of the network. In this, it is just like the hardening of those initial intuitions in a dogmatic framework that defines a clear watershed between those who are inside

3 On the movement linked to multiple personality, see Hacking (1995, pp. 58–80).

and those who are outside the movement, between friends and enemies, and those who share and those who fear its paradigm, programmes and general vision of the world.

In a climate of this kind, it is no surprise that a rapid multiplication in diagnoses at once led to growing scepticism, as these diagnoses were sometimes consolidated with the help of hypnosis or disinhibiting drugs.[4] In the growing tension between the two fronts, the breaking point came in the mid-1990s, with trials held on the basis of memories that had emerged during therapy, usually centred on sexual abuse in the early years of life. In the most famous of these cases, Gary Ramona, a Californian businessman who had been accused by his twenty-year-old daughter of sexually molesting her during childhood, in turn sued the girl's therapists for inducing false memories in her, and was awarded damages to the tune of half a million dollars.

To have a balanced picture of the whole set-up, we should emphasize that the Ramona trial did not concern a case of dissociative disorder in the strict sense (Holly Ramona was being treated for depression and bulimia), and that, analysed in detail, its outcome seems anything but clear and final.[5] In addition, its media impact at the time was helped and encouraged by another kind of social network that was no less turbid and complex – the False Memory Syndrome Foundation, set up in 1992 in Philadelphia with the precise aim of helping families involved in accusations of this kind.[6]

As is easily imaginable, the disturbing legal, economic and media repercussions that had emerged in court had the effect of scaling down the ideological fervour that had grown up around dissociative phenomena, implicitly giving back a voice

4 The somewhat casual use of sodium amytal to bring to the surface repressed traumatic memories was a constant in therapeutic treatment in the mid-1990s.

5 Actually, the jury rejected the case against the two therapists of inducing false memories in the patient, but recognized them as guilty of professional malpractice and responsible for 45% of the moral and material damage suffered by Ramona. Leaving aside a further 50% attributed to his wife (who had asked for a divorce) and his employer (who had sacked him), the remaining 5% of responsibility was assigned to Ramona for his general neglect of his children. The accusation of sexual violence towards Ramona had already been rejected in a previous hearing and was not considered in the final trial. However, Holly Ramona continued to confirm her accusations, both during the trial and after, and her mother was wholly convinced by her version of the facts.

6 At the time of the Ramona case, there were almost 20,000 such families in the USA. During the trial, the False Memory Syndrome Foundation supported the plaintiff with every possible means, succeeding in having some of its members accepted as expert witnesses in the hearing. After the precedent of Ramona, many cases pending for child abuse were either withdrawn, or concluded with an acquittal. It is worth recalling that the first leader of the foundation, the former Lutheran pastor Ralph Underwager, was removed from his position after a Dutch booklet for paedophiles published an interview with him that contained the declaration that sexual relations between adults and children enter into the "will of God". His wife Hollida Wakefield remained on the foundation's board even after that.

and influence to more solid and reliable researchers. The most significant corollary of this transition of responsibility is the now consolidated tendency to disregard the more dramatic symptoms of multiple personality, which are considered as just the extreme tip on a scale of similar manifestations of greatly varying seriousness in psychological profiles that are themselves heterogeneous. The very reclassification of the syndrome in the much more general form of *dissociative identity disorder* went in this direction, and indirectly alluded to the possibility that a primary psychic mechanism that has a basic function in the organization of the mind *in general*, and not just more or less serious pathologies, filters through in these cases. For us, the point is to understand if these strata of the problem, which clearly lie deeper, tend to dissolve or to confirm the close link between the dissociative mechanisms and the social dynamic, which so far we have hardly glanced at.

3 Denial and perversion

The history of the concept of *dissociation* is littered with translations that are not always literal, but subtle semantic modifications from one author to another that shift the centre of gravity of research towards clinical cases that are different each time. William James used "dissociation" for the term *désagrégation*, which had been introduced by Janet and rendered with *Dissoziation* by Breuer and Freud, and *hysteria* was the standard diagnosis in these early studies. A few years later, however, Bleuler was to introduce the term *Spaltung*, which was promptly translated into French as *dissociation*, to indicate the basic pathological process of *dementia praecox*, which, on the basis of this new interpretation, was renamed *schizophrenia*. As we know, Freud was unimpressed by this neologism, rejecting Bleuler's theory outright. More than twenty years later, however, he would himself reintroduce the term *Spaltung*, this time in the context of an analysis of sexual perversions, and of *fetishism* in particular. Later, in *An Outline of Psycho-Analysis*, he even developed the theory that the mechanism of *Spaltung*, which he specifically distinguished from repression, might play a central role not only in the perversions, but in the constitution of the psyche in general – a conjecture that was taken up by Lacan in his own personal re-reading of Freud's text (see Grilliat 1999). Finally, we should mention the increasing centrality of the terms "split" and "dissociation" in English-language psychoanalysis, from Melanie Klein's canonical formulations to Otto Kernberg's research on borderline personality.

However marked the differences in research perspective and the kind of pathology examined may be, it is difficult to avoid the impression that in all of them the terms "split" or "dissociation" allude to a similar psychic mechanism that comes on stage each time in a different costume and with a different accent. The mechanism would seem to consist essentially in *cutting the connections* that join one specific segment to the rest of psychic experience, creating a *watertight compartment*, an island detached from every other aspect of the personality, to the point that psychic experience becomes so fragmented as to be like an archipelago or a sum of monads, without doors or windows.

It is important to underline the difference between this dissociative mechanism and *repression* in the canonical sense. The latter, as is generally known, drives some psychic content down into the unconscious and traces a *horizontal* line of separation between the Ego and the Id as a momentary outcome of the conflict between two opposing psychic demands. In the case of dissociation, by contrast, the split operates *vertically* (Goldberg 1999): the rejected content remains fundamentally available to the consciousness, but confined in a separate region of the psychic personality, where it carries on a kind of parallel life. Once the dissociation has taken place, the very conditions of psychic conflict are eliminated at root, since the two virtually opposing demands can now coexist without clashing and therefore without the subject being forced to give up one or the other. The price for this compromise solution, however, is a laceration *within the Ego*, which can maintain its hold on the dissociated regions of psychic experience only by splitting itself.

In Freud's text this *splitting of the Ego* is bound hand and foot to a paradoxical psychic operation: *Verleugnung* (usually translated as *denial* or *disavowal*), which is very different from *denial* (*Verneinung*) in the general sense of the term. In sharp contrast with the classical logic of *repression*, which supresses the drives in the interest of the reality principle, denial is usually at the expense of *an aspect of reality* that contradicts one of the drives. The canonical example, in fetishism, is the perception of the fact that the woman (in particular, the mother) has no penis, a fact that is in sharp contrast with the child's drive towards a symbiotic fusion with the mother's body, which can set off, in Freud's view, an intolerable castration complex.

Now, in the development of fetishism, the perception of this fact is *denied*, but in a way that paradoxically involves *at the same time* both rejection and acceptance: "two contrary and independent attitudes always arise and result in the situation of there being a splitting of the ego" (Freud 1938b, p. 234).

In his *Outline* Freud makes absolutely clear that this kind of disavowal of reality is very frequent, particularly in childhood, and is certainly not limited to the case of fetishists. He had introduced the term *Verleugnung* as early as the article of 1927, in which he had cited as an example the case of two brothers who had both reacted to their father's death with a similar split of identity: "It was only one current in their mental life that had not recognized their father's death; there was another current which took full account of the fact. The attitude which fitted in with the wish and the attitude which fitted in with reality existed side by side" (Freud 1927b, p. 156). Octave Mannoni (1969) referred to the proverbial formula, "*Je sais bien, mais quand même…*" to describe this ambivalent, split attitude, the mirror opposite of the ironic justification of superstitions: "It's not true, but I believe it." The denial, as we can see, is concentrated not on the inner drive, as is the case in repression, but on the perception of reality: it is a *not-wanting-to-see*, which allows the desire to coexist, unmutilated, with a reality that, strictly speaking, should rule it out of court.

In these terms, it will not be difficult to identify its schema in the most diverse variants, both in individual experience and in collective cultural constructs. The phenomenology of psychological dependence, for example, is full of cases of splits, in which a form of behaviour that is sincerely condemned in the light of day is regularly and unhesitatingly reproduced at nightfall (Caretti and Di Cesare 2005). Similarly, on the cultural side, the science of religions is familiar with collective rituals that usually set up an illusionistic world, whose intrinsic ambivalence reflects the denial of negativity in its various forms: finiteness, death, the threatening of an uncontrolled nature, and so on.[7] It is not without significance that Steiner (1993) has suggested we re-read in terms of denial Sophocles's *Oedipus Rex*, an emblem, at least for the psychoanalytic tradition, of the intermixing of the story of an individual and a collective cultural development. Without questioning the almost universal range of the problem, however, it is worth pausing a moment on the exemplary case of fetishism, to focus more clearly the various aspects of the work of dissociation.

As we have seen, the fetishist's problem lies in mediating between his drive and reality – we might say, between the inner and outer world – so as to eliminate any potential conflict. The synthesis between the two demands, however, happens in a dimension that, strictly speaking, is neither psychic nor real, neither *inner* nor *outer*. It is that of the *fetish*, usually a real object "lent" to the imagination, where it can take on the fictitious role of the female penis: an item of underwear, a high heel, a jewel, or some other more remote material feature that is linked unconsciously to the discovery and denial of the female organ. In any case, it is, quite literally, a *cache-sexe*.

According to Freud, the introduction of this third realm, halfway between reality and representation, is an extraordinarily "artful" and "ingenious" stratagem. Not only does it allow the fetishist to remain true to his desire, refusing to sacrifice it to reality, but it even ensures his satisfaction, which "other men have to woo and make exertions for" (Freud 1927b, p. 154). While being a real object, the fetish is always available, and can effortlessly materialize at any moment, *exactly like a representation*.[8]

Obviously, the weak point in this operation is that the liminal dimension in which it takes place is intrinsically fictitious: it must *count* as something real, without *being* real. To function, the theatre of the perversion must therefore *isolate itself* from reality and organize itself as a separate, protected space – a *niche*, indeed, in which the game has special rules. At the same time, however, this niche cannot be wholly reduced to a merely mental space of pure representation: it must maintain an ambiguous position, some *claim to reality*, if it is successfully to keep at bay the distress that, from the start, has imposed and goes on imposing the denial of what is known to be the "true" reality. The simplest way of maintaining

7 I take the expression "illusionistic world" from Pruyser (1985), who in turn was influenced by Freud (1927).

8 One striking example cited by Freud is that of a patient who had chosen as his fetish a certain type of "shine on the nose", with which the subject clearly endowed at will the women he decided to court (Freud 1927b, p. 152).

this pseudo-reality is to obtain the *consent of someone else*, or, more precisely, their complicity in *joining in the game*. It is needless to add that this complicity, when it occurs, will be obtained with threats, blackmail or other more or less explicit forms of coercion: the internal overtones of perversion, its hovering between a contract and an act of violence, are subjects that can be left for another time. What is essential, for the moment, is this preliminary account of the mechanism presiding over the setting up of a psychic niche: the creation of a realm that lies between reality and representation, and the need to confirm its ambivalent status through the complicity of another who will join in the game. The point is to understand what form these two structural features acquire, outside the specific domain of the perversion, in marking out other niches, defined by clearer social and collective conditions.

4 Primary dissociation

Freud notes in his explanation of the paradoxical nature of denial that the two contrary attitudes – accepting and rejecting a perception of the real – only coexist in it thanks to the mechanisms of the "primary process" in the development of the mind, which is much more ancient and remote than the logical rules that structure human languages in their evolved forms. The most recent studies, based both on clinical experience and on direct observation of child behaviour, confirm this picture incontrovertibly, and, following a path opened up by Melanie Klein, tend to relate the origin of the dissociative mechanism to the early months of life – that is to say, in a phase *preceding* language acquisition. In this light, denial in the true sense might be just a reflection, in a now-linguistic dimension, of an older, *pre-symbolic* defence mechanism, rooted in the most obscure phase of our psychic development – when the speaking animal is, quite literally, an *in-fant*, already containing the pure potentiality of language, yet still without words.

The starting point for understanding, even hypothetically, the significance of this primary mechanism of childhood dissociation, is the requisite that, research confirms, is the dominant feature of psychic experience in the first year of life – the *lack* of distinction between inner and outer, *representation* and *fact*, which in later phases becomes the necessary premise of any genuine *symbolic* function. In a small child's world every drive, emotion or desire belongs at once to reality, while every perception of the real is, at the same time, part of the inner life of the psyche. Paraphrasing one of Wittgenstein's (1930, VI, p. 58) thought experiments, we might say that it is an existential dimension where "there is pain" or "there is thought", just as there is a roll of thunder or a downpour, and this *psychic equivalence*, which seems to define the *earliest* human experience of being in the world, is bound to leave its traces in all later phases of psychic development, coexisting, perhaps *sotto voce*, with the development of language and the symbolic faculty.

That psychic equivalence marks a *pre-symbolic* form of mental organization does not mean, however, that we should treat it as a pre-human and generally animal dimension. On the contrary, everything suggests that it is only possible biologically as a preliminary to language development, and so in a specifically human evolutionary framework. Further: recent studies on human cognition, from linguistics to artificial intelligence, tend to suggest that the two levels – the symbolic and sub-symbolic ones – do not simply succeed one another in individual psychic development, but *coexist* and can only function in a system of interchange and constant interpenetration that has no equivalent in other living species without the faculty of language. This is clearly repeating an intuition familiar to psychoanalysis, and also, in its main lines, to much of the European philosophical tradition. Nevertheless, the actual details and the dynamic of this mixture of the symbolic and sub-symbolic, which marks all human experience of thought, are still largely unknown. It seems that it is precisely in this unknown region, *on the borders* of the symbolic and sub-symbolic, that the *primary* moment of the dissociative processes should be located.

This aspect can be decisive for the problems that concern us. If there really is a dialectic between language and our drives that marks the human psyche *specifically*, then it is likely that its configuration will restate more clearly the anthropological paradox, which, for the moment, we are familiar with only in its formal schema. This would confirm our hypothesis that dissociative phenomena give access to this basic crux of the human condition. However, to flesh out this delicate speculative transition, we should extend our angle of vision and go back to the anthropological considerations already advanced in the first chapter, to suggest a version that is closer to the problems we are discussing.

We have already noted at the outset that a living organism is not usually exposed to the world indiscriminately. The stimuli to which it reacts are those that a long process of adaptation has selected as indispensable for survival; the rest are either not perceived as such at all or are at once dismissed as mere *noise*. The concept of *environment* (*Umwelt*) proposed by Uexküll had the precise function of marking the decisive importance of this separation between signal and noise – between what is biologically *significant* for an organism and therefore already inscribed in a system of instinctual programmes, and what is excluded as mere noise from the environmental niche to which it is destined. This correlation organism/environment has, of course, various modalities and overtones, and it becomes richer and more flexible in more complex organisms, which are receptive to input from individual experience and learning. As far as we know, however, the distinction between signal and noise remains in non-human animals the *premise* for any further extension of its environmental horizons. There is no animal species that can be exposed to a wholly chaotic, undifferentiated flux of information without a system of innate instincts selecting what *may* have meaning for it, thus reducing disorder, the unforeseen, and the contingency of exposure to the world.

By contrast, at least if we stick with the picture offered by twentieth-century philosophical anthropology, the human condition seems to be defined by a tendency *not to distinguish* between signal and noise, and, thus, by a system of *unlimited contingency.* Unlike an animal environment, the human world is constituted in such a way that nothing in it is significant on principle and everything can become so in certain conditions.

In my view, reformulating the conceptual distinction between environment and world in this way, and presenting it more soberly as a distinction between two different (not necessarily opposing) modalities for processing information, we should be able to avoid the opacity and ideological drift that have affected this anthropological approach. In other words, it is essential to distinguish the *naturalistic* content in this distinction from any tacit claim of the human animal being supposedly supra-natural. We may also need to make clear, incidentally, that though confusion between the two aspects is sometimes due to authors such as Gehlen, Plessner or even Heidegger, on other occasions it is the outcome of the scientistic approach of their critics that has little time for nuance.

Take, for example, Gehlen's schematic formula, by which the human condition can be described as *reduction of instincts* associated with *excess drives.* Taken literally, the formula expresses a naturalistic theory: that the programmed link between certain trigger stimuli and precise motor sequences tends to become more indefinite and flexible in man's psychic development, while a potential of free energy accumulates alongside, which may influence stimuli that are not part of a programme, and that set up a world of new meanings. On this view, what is essential is the *correlation* between two moments: nothing can be fully affected by the drive if it is not at the same time uncoupled from the rigidity of the instinctive mechanisms. Nothing, then, will enter the symbolic network of the world if it is not virtually uprooted from its environment and given over to absolute *contingency* – even (*above all*, indeed) the ties and needs imposed by the natural set-up only enter into the cultural construction of the "world" through the narrow door of their *deniability*, whether actual or imaginary. However, to speak of a "reduction of the instincts" in this technical sense does not mean that we have no nature, as one humanistic commonplace would have it, or that our genetic configuration is incomplete, vague or inadequate. On the contrary, a much greater biological and neuronal complexity is very probably required to obtain this difficult balance of the drives, and a sophisticated, calibrated apparatus of innate genetic programmes to allow such an extensive and flexible receptiveness. In other words, it is precisely *human nature* – if we want to use such an ambiguous term – that imposes on us the need to deal with a chaotic, undifferentiated flux, thus acquiring the possibility – and the *burden* – of setting up a system of cultural meanings. The point is that though this burden is rooted in the nature of the human animal, it is intimately paradoxical, as it constantly requires us to set up a confine between signal and noise, *starting from their indistinctness.*

Evidently, full acquisition of a natural language is the decisive step in achieving this primary biological task. In its way, this acquisition *reproduces* a system of unlimited contingency, if we take the term "contingent" in its classical sense, to indicate "what is, but could also not be". In logical terms, a language system is based on the principle that *everything* that can be said can also be *negated*:

communicating linguistically about something therefore must always mean communicating about its possible negation, and therefore about its *contingent* character. However, once exposure to the world has been reshaped by language, the subject is set in a coherent network of grammatical constraints and symbolic ties that collective communication can constantly reproduce, correct and renew, but only on the premise of a stable distinction between external reality and the inner life of its representations. We shall consider later the speculative problems and latent paradoxes in this premise of symbolic communication. What is important for the moment is to bring out that *before* this decisive step is taken, the psychic equivalence that dominates childhood experience is the exact correlate of the primary indistinctness of signal and noise, meaning that the implicit paradoxes in the task of "constructing a world" still openly manifest their explosive potential.

First of all, it is no wonder that observations, direct or indirect, of infant psychic development agree in seeing a connection between psychic equivalence and a basic annihilation anxiety, which is destined in any case to activate the first defence mechanisms and, in certain circumstances (serious deprivation, for example), opens the way to pathology. The infant's inability to distinguish between inner and outer reproduces the unfiltered exposure to the chaotic flux of the world, which is the premise of the symbolic faculty, but also the tangible sign of the *threat* that bears down on an organism that is still utterly immature, yet already catapulted into the world, with neither an adequate instinctual shield nor the protection that full possession of symbols provides. The main defence mechanism in this delicate phase of development will therefore consist of tracing each time a momentary confine – and therefore one that is both *sharp* and *precarious* – between signal and noise, obtaining that minimum degree of order within which the integrative functions correlated with the symbolic faculty can mature. It is this mechanism, so indispensable to the emerging Ego, yet still weakly differentiated to face annihilation anxiety, that we give the name of *primary dissociation*, regarding it as the origin and prototype of every piece of psychic niche-forming, or every "psychic retreat", to use Steiner's (1993) effective term.

However, what is the actual dynamic of a retreat of this kind? Clearly, it means expelling every contingency, every threateningly uncontrollable aspect of the outside world, so that the retreat's interior can be modelled as far as possible on a perfect, secure environment whose imagined ideal is life in the uterus. Taken literally, however, this ideal fusion is nothing more than the complete lack of distinction between inner and outer – that will be an idealized recreation *of psychic equivalence itself*, of the undifferentiated, unfiltered flux, from which protection was originally sought. In short, the retreat is the threat itself in idealized form. One flees *towards* what one flees *from*, and there may be no human desire that does not carry with it a trace of this ambivalence, which does not therefore require an art to neutralize and govern its internal paradox, an *art* whose general outline is traced by primary dissociation.

5 Psychic dissociation and anthropological paradox

It would be wise at this point to draw up a provisional balance and conclude this first limited reconnaissance of the terrain of psychopathology, and move on to considering other, more general aspects of the forms of life in the present.

First, in the light of our reflections so far, we can reasonably suppose that, however they may vary in their external forms and in the seriousness of the pathology, all dissociative disorders are connected to the defence mechanism of primary dissociation and its persistence, more or less marked, in an adult psyche that is now structured in symbolic forms. Without denying the varied forms dissociation may take, it may be legitimate to describe a *dissociated personality* as having four basic features:

- a fragile Ego, unprepared to bear and symbolically articulate conflict;
- an experience of external reality as essentially a destructive *threat*, connected to a basic annihilation anxiety;
- *defensive* compartmentalization of experience, dominated by a *symbiotic* desire disposed to constitute "psychic retreats" (Steiner 1993), an ambiguous third realm between facts and representations;
- masking of the fragmentary, partial character of these dissociated compartments by systematic recourse to denial and fiction, tending to obscure the confine between reality and illusion.

That a similar profile can be found in a growing percentage of clinical cases seems confirmed by the statistics and the specialist literature. That, outside medical studies, it may be regarded as a typical way of being in our times is what mass culture and, in some respects, everyday experience suggest. Even given these premises, it is still difficult to establish beyond doubt whether dissociative attitudes are actually more widespread today than a few decades ago, or whether it is the interpretative models that have changed – the interpretative schemas with which doctors, newspapers and institutions describe situations and cases that would once have been categorized differently. From our point of view, this could be, at bottom, a false alternative. The construction of psychic identity and the development of social sensibility are not two distinct phenomena at all, but two poles of the same process of cultural reproduction, joined by a thick web of references and a kind of *resonance* that is precisely what we are to investigate. In the first section on multiple personality, we barely sounded the most superficial aspects of this resonance, but now, as the deeper strata gradually emerge, the problem takes on vastly more extensive dimensions.

Meanwhile, it has been ascertained that primary dissociation, in itself, is not at all a pathological dysfunction, but an essential psychic mechanism that performs a constructive function in the development of the mind *in general.* At first, what sets off this mechanism is the need to protect oneself from an undifferentiated flux of stimuli in which *nothing* has a prescribed, once-and-for-all, biological meaning, but *everything* can acquire one, if it happens to channel onto itself the input of a drive that is naturally flexible and therefore essentially unpredictable. Paradoxically, however, dissociation cannot protect us from this unlimited contingency except by attaching itself to the psychic equivalence that is responsible for the world seeming so threatening, making it the exclusive feature of a niche that is rigidly separated and protected from external reality.

In the mature phases of psychic development, language acquisition stabilizes, at least in principle, the distinction between external reality and internal representations, opening the way to more structured forms for protecting the Ego's identity. However, the paradox is not eliminated: it remains the hinge on which the dialectic between language and drives revolves, between a symbolic plane and a sub-symbolic plane that, together, define the organization of the mind and the forms of life of the human animal.

This seems to confirm the hypothesis that dissociative disorders carry traces of the complex dynamic of the "anthropological paradox". Indeed, by reconstructing the deepest element of dissociation we can trace more precisely the features of this paradoxical dynamic, at least in its psychological aspect. However, not only does the correlation with the social plane remain obscure for the moment, apart from the most superficial aspects of the phenomenon, but there is an underlying difficulty that prevents us from leaping too hastily to general conclusions.

As psychopathology describes them, forms of dissociation fundamentally display a *failure* of psychic strategies, in which the defensive modality prevails and the mind seems unable to make sense of its internal paradoxes. If we are to give an account that really does have general anthropological value, then we cannot just surreptitiously extend these models to the more stable and successful forms of life, leaving their substance unaltered. Rather, we must suppose that psychiatry is familiar with just *one* possible version of primary dissociation, but that there is also another, perhaps less recognizable at first sight precisely because it can be consolidated in forms of psychic existence that are adequate to the need to give form to the world.

Let us not forget, though, that this primary anthropological task inevitably involves the psychic mechanisms just as much as the social systems and the large collective institutions, which means that, on this terrain, the interpenetration between the two planes is decisive for both. We know, however, that, in the *specifically modern* response to the problem, the dominant model of social rationality rested on the repression of the drives and subordination to the law, imposed a sharp horizontal break between the symbolic and sub-symbolic planes, and thus effectively restricted genuine dissociation to the infant parenthesis alone. In this context, it was inevitable that the psychic construction of a niche seemed not just distinct from, but *antithetical* to the construction of a cultural world: a dangerous form of infantilism and ineptitude, a flight from a dysfunctional and pathological reality.

We shall see in the next chapter how dubious and inadequate this traditional point of view may prove to be. Meanwhile, it is worth noting that the emergence of a different collective sensibility might become at this point the gauge of a much deeper cultural phenomenon than just a higher or lower statistical distribution of some pathology. At the risk of oversimplifying, let us hazard a general hypothesis that can act as a guide in what follows: that there has been a displacement of the resonance between social processes and psychic mechanisms in this period. While the modern institutions resonated naturally with the repression of the drives, linked to a deployment of symbolic laws, we might say that *the late-modern social networks tend to link up with dissociative mechanisms*, thus shifting interpenetration to a deeper and more elusive plane that seems to be the hinge between the symbolic and sub-symbolic levels.

Without questioning in the least the (at present) wholly hypothetical nature of this construct, let us try asking: what would the *sense* be of such a change in the forms of life? What might its most likely *causes* be? And what its most significant consequences?

Chapter 3

The grey area between fact and fiction

> Learn from little children, who first play the game and then believe in it.
>
> Luigi Pirandello, *I giganti della montagna*

I Illusion, reality and play

In the previous chapter, I conjectured that the psychic mechanism of primary dissociation plays a constructive role in the economy of the human mind *in general*. If there is anything in this, we should expect the dissociative state, which I have described in general terms, to be widespread, and recognizable beyond the confines of pathology. The dissociative disorders described by psychiatrists should be seen, in short, as the extreme form – or internal risk – of a possible structure of the mind that is not necessarily pathological or dysfunctional in itself.

Now, the real difficulty is that a hypothesis of this kind does not simply make some minor adjustments to the conventional boundary between normality and deviance, but profoundly questions the whole conception of the relation between psychic and social planes that has been transmitted to us by modern culture. In the classical "modern" perspective, the traits of the dissociative personality all seem synonymous with inevitable *social dysfunctionality* rather than pathology. Unable to deal with conflict and ready to take refuge in a mixture of reality and illusion, the dissociated subject seems, by definition, unsuited for any serious productive task. In addition, his propensity to break up experience into so many separate compartments makes him *disloyal* in principle, unable to subordinate himself to a coherent law and take on any stable social responsibility. On these premises, the mere hypothesis that the dissociative mechanisms can *also* perform a constructive function and, in certain conditions, *positively* participate in the processes of constructing the cultural world will – inevitably and understandably – come up against various objections.

The most serious of these, in my view, is that a dissociative practice will inevitably tend to lead to a *fetish*, a hybrid between reality and representation, designed to repudiate the distressing aspects of the outside world. Even if we accept that illusions of this kind are sometimes functional to social stability, as has often been the case in the religious tradition, it seems to require remarkable naivety or cynicism to see such flights from reality as having a constructive value existentially and culturally. This is an absolutely legitimate objection, whose strength lies in combining two different levels of argument, one *moral* and the other *theoretical*. The first is summed up in the opposition between illusion and reality, which may define the supreme value of modern enlightenment, of which Freud himself is one of the most authoritative custodians. In the Enlightenment tradition, the full acquisition of the reality principle, despite the frustration of our narcissistic illusions that is implicit in it, is usually considered a decisive threshold onto maturity – culturally, historically and otherwise – and, in clear contradiction with the religious tradition, is seen as crowning the process of civilization (Freud 1927). The theoretical foundation of this conception, however, is the distinction between inner and outer world, between *representations* and *facts*, which, as we have seen, is usually recognized as the foundation of verbal language and, more generally, of our species' symbolic faculty. It is because it identifies with this unquestioned threshold of *psychic* maturity that the modern rejection of illusions can be compared to cultural maturity, thus helping consolidate the opposition between *civilization* and *barbarity* in its specifically modern sense. We must now see if this foundation really stands up, or whether, at bottom, the classical values of modern morality, such as "renouncing illusions" and "adapting to reality", are not more opaque than at first appears.

Actually, we shall soon see that, in the main philosophical theories on the foundations of language, this oh-so-basic distinction between inner and outer proves to be anything but straightforward and unproblematic. However, even if we limit ourselves to psychic development for the moment, the *genesis* of this distinction is a complex problem. In his psychoanalytical work on small children, D.W. Winnicott showed that in the acquisition of this symbolic threshold, the decisive role is played by a "third area" (Winnicott 1971, p. 102) that is neither psychic innerness nor external reality, but rather an "intermediate area", a "potential space" that contains both of them. This area is first manifested in *transitional objects*, "the intermediate area of experience, between the thumb and the teddy bear" (Winnicott 1971, p. 2), peopled by special objects that are particularly precious to the child and that "are not part of the infant's body yet are not fully recognized as belonging to external reality" (Winnicott 1971, p. 3). Evidently, this dual citizenship of transitional objects involves a paradox. The crucial point in Winnicott's theory, however, is that "the paradox needs to be accepted, tolerated, and not resolved" (Winnicott 1971, p. 53): "of the transitional object it can be said that it is a matter of agreement between us and the baby that we will never ask the question: 'Did you conceive of this or was it presented to you from without?' The important point is that no decision on this point is expected. The question is not to be formulated" (Winnicott 1971, p. 17).

This subtle combination of latent paradox and collective complicity returns in the more complete and anthropologically exemplary development of the transitional phenomenon: the *play* space in which the "pretend mode" is in control. Here too everyone must "join in the game", tacitly refraining from raising the question of the status of the reality or pretence involved in what is taking place. To this end, it is particularly necessary for the play space to be carefully delimited and separated from outside reality, and, in their reworking of Winnicott's theory, Fonagy and Target (2000) rightly underline the meticulous patience and care with which children apply themselves to this in the preliminary phase, which often requires more time and effort than the game itself. According to Fonagy and Target, the importance of this separation lies in the fact that the pretend mode takes shape in a phase in which the child's world is still to a large extent dominated by psychic equivalence, which confers immediate reality on every kind of fantasy, desire or representation. In the delimited, artificial space of the pretend mode, fantasies and desires can have free rein, precisely because any link with potential consequences is suspended. Hence the serious pathogenic effect of any irruption of the real into the play space, as in typical cases of seduction and abuse.

These brief notes should suffice to indicate that the transitional area and its development in children's games are *a precise mirror image of the work of dissociation*, which reproduces all of its structural aspects. These are the creation of a protective niche, the sharp separation from the outside, the paradoxical combination of reality and illusion, which tends to concentrate in a fetish, and the crucial value of the complicity and assent of someone else for the success of the whole construction. It is no surprise, then, that Fonagy and Target themselves note the connection, observing that "a key part of dissociation as a phenomenon is the re-emergence of the pretend mode, the mode in which the very young child fully enters a separate psychic world, and cannot simultaneously maintain contact with ordinary reality" (Fonagy and Target 2000, p. 864).

In the experience of play, however, marking out a niche is not functional to denying reality, but to *mastering* it. For a game to function, for it to succeed in channelling and sublimating the drives, the deepest, most disturbing and potentially threatening aspects of the real situation must "come into play". The space marked out for the game, then, is not a repudiation of reality, but a *projection* of it in the framework of conventional rules that limit contingency and encourage the selection of more effective responses. Now, everyone knows the power of the spell that has always been cast by the model of the game as a paradigm of cultural creativity, usually associated with a melancholy awareness of its fragility, from which follows the fact that no game can last long. One might say that both its charm and its fragility depend on the fact that while this delicate projection continues to be successful, it creates the ideal conditions for *dealing with both polarities of the anthropological paradox at a stroke*. The reassuring perimeter of the rules selects and screens the absolute contingency of the outside world; but the fact that it is precisely the most disturbing features of the real world that are projected onto this screen generates an openness, a possibility of contact that can gradually extend to complete mastery.

In all this, the underlying difficulty is that a compromise is not good enough, because, as we know, the two aspirations are linked by a paradoxical constraint that is far more complex than mere opposition. The logical space set up by the game is thus bound to absorb this paradoxical dynamic, only to reproduce it every time in every variation and, more generally, in every practice of the symbolic faculty modelled on the paradigm of play. First, as we have said, it is a condition of playing that it *includes* the disturbing aspects of external reality and at the same time *neutralizes them*, limiting their contingency to the relatively harmless possibilities envisaged by the rules. However, precisely because they are conventions, these rules *are contingent too*: they must be explained and discussed, they can be accepted or rejected, and they may even change *during* the game for it to proceed as desired. So, what limits contingency is itself, deep down, contingent too, and this circularity situates the player in an intimately split position, both inside and outside the logical space of the game, protected and exposed to the contingency of the real.

We shall have the opportunity later to measure the incidence of these paradoxes in every other case of "successful" dissociation. For now, let us simply note that, in this case, it is the internal fragility of the whole construction, not a predestined flight to pathology, that imposes the split with external reality. Rather, as we have already noted, the pathological break is set off when the real world irrupts into the niche, opening the gates to psychic equivalence. In short, it is not dissociation itself that is the pathogenic factor, but, if anything, *its failure*.

2 Successful and unsuccessful dissociations

The example of *play*, as we can see, suggests a reading of the relation between dissociation and pathology that completely overturns the traditional point of view. Recognizing the dissociative attitude as having a constructive value is, in this case, absolutely logical, and nothing excludes the possibility of a similar picture reappearing in other contexts, including those of adult life. This is, in fact, the general line of the various recent attempts to identify a *"successful" dissociation* alongside or underlying its pathological degeneration.[1] It is no accident, then, that all of them, more or less explicitly, take up Winnicott's interpretation of children's play. A rehabilitation of the dissociative mechanisms as a principle of mental organization and the consequent evaluation of their emergence in present-day forms of life that is not simply negative depends essentially on the value that we attribute to the play area as an intimately paradoxical logical space in the mature functioning of our symbolic faculty. In slightly more emphatic terms, we might say they depend on the anthropological significance we give to childhood, where playing is the primary mode of experience. We might consider *childhood* a phase of development that should be completely left behind once we are fully able to organize the symbolic faculty, or, alternatively, think that even the mature form of this faculty cannot achieve its full potential without remaining profoundly and constantly in touch with a *child's* mode of mental organization, linking the symbolic and sub-symbolic planes.

1 See Goldberg (1995), Bromberg (1996).

In Winnicott's model, the response to this dilemma leaves no room for doubt. The logical space of the play area, with its paradoxical refusal to distinguish between inner and outer, is explicitly offered as the necessary key for binding representations to facts, and so as the prototype of any culturally significant experience, starting with art and religion (see Winnicott 1971, pp. 18–19). For Winnicott, more especially, play is the prototype of all *creative* behaviour, precisely because creativity involves the paradox of a transformation of the rules *while playing*, even though it is those very rules that make the game possible.

With this reference to "creativity", we open the gates to a whole cultural tradition, which sees in this faculty of *creating the new* the most distinctive expression of our humanity. One could easily retrace it along the whole parabola of modernity, from the primacy of *wit* (*ingenium*) in the Renaissance, via the theory of *genius* in German idealism, down to the anthropology of creativity developed by American pragmatism (see Joas 1992). In all these experiences of thought, what is at stake is a conception of human nature and the process of civilization that is openly alternative to the cornerstones of the dominant paradigm, which rejects *both* the repression of the drives as necessary for controlling them properly, *and* the universality and primacy of the law as the formal expression of rationality. No discourse on modernity and its eclipse can ignore this alternative tradition, without falling into an abstract, unproductive schematism, and so, logically, our enquiry should consider this argument.

Here and in the following chapters, I shall therefore try to bring out the alternation between *successful* or *unsuccessful* forms of dissociation, considering in each case whether they can interact functionally with the social and communicative context, contribute creatively to establishing reality, or simply deny it, and, more generally, whether or not they succeed in dealing with the anthropological paradox. As I have already made clear, I shall be referring essentially to the *contemporary* context, with its specific historical features. However, this aspect of modernity that presents itself under the general banner of "creativity" is alternative to the dominant model and appeals to a different anthropological conception. Inevitably, then, two factors must be briefly mentioned here, as, though they are far removed from the present forms of life, they help illuminate their meaning. These are *ritual* practice, to which, as we have seen, we can attribute a primary anthropological meaning, and the *genesis of modernity*, in which, as we know, dissociative attitudes were decisively excluded from "normal" forms of correlation between the psychic and social planes. Before venturing down this path, however, there is a critical reflection to be made.

Precisely because it is offered as an alternative to the dominant paradigm, the anthropological conception based on creativity tended in the twentieth century to be presented in essentially *utopian* terms. Rather than being translated into actual existential practices, it countered existing forms of life with an *ideal* alternative that, to perform its critical function, often clad itself self-defensively in the clothes of daydreaming. At the turn of the century, the crisis of the modern world thus came as a rude awakening. Although the emerging forms of life are freer of the constraints imposed in the past, and although creativity and imagination play an increasingly central role in the main social practices associated with them, the overall effect of this eclipse of modernity has proved decidedly less liberating than some thinkers once expected.

A link between creative practice and psychic dissociation, like that which has emerged from these brief remarks on the example of play, can only emphasize this inevitable farewell to utopia. The dissociative mechanisms are and remain essentially *defensive* strategies, tied to an experience of the world marked by danger, fear and negativity. So, even if we accept that they reveal the possibility of "successful" practices – ones that are functional and adequate to the social dynamic – their frame of reference cannot be so idyllic, given that it activates so intensely the demand for *protection*. We should never forget, when drawing up a critical balance sheet, that modern institutions have offered a response to this desire that has proved to be particularly stable and successful. With their decline, the need for protection and security certainly does not disappear, but only shifts towards different complexes and strategies, not "better" in the abstract, but simply more suited to an historically different context.

Though the optimism of utopia risks being misleading, we should not assume that systematic pessimism is in itself a guarantee of objectivity. We know that dissociations, whether successful or unsuccessful, are linked, in a form that still needs investigating, to social development, which, in the last century, gradually eroded the hierarchical order to the advantage of a network of "vertical splits", in which groups and environments that are profoundly heterogeneous find themselves coexisting on the same plane. It seemed obvious to the first and most profound observers of this new state of affairs – thinkers like Schmitt, Gehlen or Heidegger himself – that the *pluralism* of mass democracies was the political correlate of this development. The more radical their critical approach, then, the greater the risk of criticism opening the way to political experiments that were overtly illiberal, with the aim of restoring the homogeneity of the people and the sovereignty of its guides by any means. With hindsight, it was all too easy to reject this path, whose failure is notorious. However, it is more difficult to dismiss its foundations, reading these phenomena not as worrying signals of decline but as the emergence of a primary anthropological crux that, however complex and ambivalent it may be, may find more transparent and authentic expression today than that provided by the more traditional forms of life and social organization in their time.

In short, as we can see if we are realistic, an evaluation of the present has to perform a difficult balancing act that recognizes both the light and shade of the present historical contingency, without any ideological prejudice tipping the balance one way or another. To avoid a limitingly partial vision of this kind, I intend to present my argument in a somewhat unorthodox way. I am going to start from the general and the abstract, which will serve as a background for *all* the phenomenal ambits that we shall be examining – and that is the *lack of distinction between facts and representations*. This method – let it be said at once – will make the following pages seem speculative and, hence, more than a little schematic. In the following chapters, though, we shall be able to gradually transfer this scheme onto the firm ground of empirical reality, so as to distinguish there its various facets with a clearer understanding of the facts.

3 Performativity and social networks

So far, we have considered the indistinctness between facts and representations as a *pre-symbolic* characteristic linked to the childhood phase of psychic development. This may have suggested that the *symbolic* dimension in the strict sense – that in which both "rational" mental acts and socially significant operations are considered – rests on a distinction between facts and representations that is now stable, final and freed of any opacity or blind spots. However, if we pass from the psychological register to that of a general theory of language and representation, this tacit assumption starts to look dubious, if not wholly unfounded.

Gottlob Frege, for example, the father of modern analytical philosophy, was convinced that this distinction could only be coherent if we acknowledge a "third realm": that of real *thoughts* as distinguished from facts, because not part of the sensible world, but also distinguished from representations, because *logical*, not *psychological*, entities, timeless, without a subject, and existing in themselves for themselves. Frege's Platonism may be an exception in modern thought, though it is less rare than one might think; it is, in any case, an attempt to provide a final answer to a difficulty that constantly makes itself felt in all speculative thinking on language. The point is that it is hard to prevent the distinction between facts and representations dissolving or being completely *absorbed* in one or other of its two polarities, forcing us to admit with equal cogency either that, really, there are only facts, or that everything is representation.

We all know that, in the end, our only access to external reality is through representations, starting with those of our senses, and that it is only from these representations that we can extract, often partially or distortedly, the image of a supposed "objective" reality. On this premise, we may soon reach the conclusion that, in the end, there are no facts, but *only* representations. On the other hand, what makes something a "representation" in the usual sense – an image, a picture, or a written phrase – is a factual reality: the *fact*, that is, that the colours or ink marks are arranged in a certain order. We need only extend the idea to *inner* representations – seeing them, for example, as a certain arrangement of mental symbols or, at most, circuits and connections of neurons – to conclude that, in the end, there are only *facts*, and the distinction between facts and representations is just a superficial and illusory construct.

Arguments of this kind, which can be summarily labelled *solipsism* and *physicalism*, have been reworked any number of times in the history of thought ever since the speculative challenge of the sophists in the ancient world. As in the *topoi* of classical rhetoric, it matters little how far one moves each time from the basic argument plan and, above all, it matters little that they seem at first sight to be on opposite sides. At bottom, both are following the same aim of shaking the premise of the symbolic order, which is reduced to a mere surface shell, so as to bring out a deep-seated ontological dimension that cannot be reduced to conventional logic and rationality. It is no surprise, then, that these two extremes often rubbed shoulders at crucial historical moments of particular tension: in Plato's and Aristotle's efforts to distinguish the new philosophical knowledge from both Sophism and the Pre-Socratic tradition; in Descartes's hypothesis of the "malignant demon"; or in the foundation of modern formal logic in thinkers such as Frege or Russell.

Given the enormous historical distance separating these speculative experiments, it is risky to try to seek a common denominator. However, at least on the *stylistic* level, we cannot fail to note that physicalism and solipsism are usually cited in these cases more as *intellectual challenges* than as genuine theories. It would seem that in the past people found it difficult to believe that someone might *really* want to reduce all facts to representations or vice versa, to the point of undermining the premises of symbolic logic and rational argument. The problem was more one of thinking out an adequate refutation of such radical hypotheses, one that would leave no logical foothold. Usually, as in the classical argument against scepticism, the decisive move consisted in showing that in destabilizing the foundations of logical discourse, positions of this kind ended up demolishing their *own* foundations too, thus proving to be empty scholastic exercises.

Now, without wishing to enter too far into this kind of metaphysical dispute, let us simply note that the *tone* of the problem in the culture of the present seems decidedly different. For one thing, it is well known that these radical ideas were central to the thought of such leading philosophers as Nietzsche and Wittgenstein, not just as sceptical provocations, but as basic conditions for thought that would truly break free of the limitations of the metaphysical tradition. Still more important than this change of direction in speculative theory is that the principle of the lack of distinction between facts and representations has for some time now become *an operative premise in much advanced techno-scientific research*, a premise that becomes all the more significant and profound, the less it has to be explicitly formulated.

Any technical manipulation of information, such as transferring it from one medium to another, naturally works on the *factual* nature of the representations, and it is tacitly confirmed in all the human techno-sciences, from robotics to the neurosciences, that research in this area must gradually be extended to *inner* representations. Nor are there any limits in principle to the possibility of intervening on representations *as facts*. At the same time, all communication science revolves around the possibility of technically manipulating the forms of transmitting and receiving what happens, and even being able to completely alter its meaning and social value. It is a good rule to be concerned about the possible (daily) misuse of these techniques of disinformation in social practices, from advertising to political propaganda. At the same time, however, it is tacitly acknowledged that there are no limits in principle – but only technical or moral limits – to this possibility of intervening on facts *as representations*.

As I have already said, it is not essential for this orientation of the techno-sciences to explicitly favour any specific ontological option and, when this happens, it is surprising how little the logical arguments of the past are modified, apart from technical jargon and examples with a science-fiction flavour.[2] In itself, then, the fact that physicalism and solipsism may now define the conceptual background of the techno-sciences does not make them any more epistemologically plausible, but that is not the decisive point. In the past, too, refuting them was actually, at bottom, more *practical* than logical. As the indistinctness between reality and representation was the equivalent of the demolition of all certain, effective and meaningful knowledge, it was perceived essentially as a *threat* that risked disturbing any socially significant communication, from the transmission of substantiated knowledge to peaceful forms of political debate. It was a threat, then, for *social* reproduction, still more than for the validity of the theories. On the contrary, one might say that with the growth of technology, present-day social practices tend to permanently settle *in the grey area where facts and representations become confused*, and that this confusion has become the *humus* that the social networks need, if they are to reproduce and thrive.

The importance of this last aspect for our argument is clear. We know that, from the start, the dissociative mechanisms were correlated with the impossibility of steadily distinguishing facts from representations. Now, if the major change brought about by the new technologies is indeed the reproduction of this impossibility on the *social* plane, then the incidence of psychic dissociation in the contemporary forms of life inevitably acquires a significance that can no longer be dismissed as mere pathology. On the other hand, to put some flesh on a reading of this kind, we would need to reconstruct in detail the complex links between developments in technology and those in the social institutions and the economic forms of production, and, clearly, an enterprise of this kind is way beyond our scope. We must therefore limit ourselves to considering a single type, which I hope may plausibly seem to have some *exemplary* value.

Following a path that has been traced since the first European reconstructions of the "post-modern condition" in the 1970s (see Lyotard 1979), I would like to give special weight to the phenomenon of *informatization*, which, in the last few decades, has assumed a more and more decisive role in all the main sectors of social life. By this term I refer to a use of technology that is designed to replace *practical* operations with *symbolic* ones, which resolves any action by manipulating symbols, while the material aspects are reduced to a mere, insignificant residue. As is well known, this trend has been with us since research began on artificial intelligence, and defines in the strict sense the fundamental aim of *robotics*, which, significantly, is

2 Recently, popularizing accounts of the cognitive sciences were fascinated for several years by the film *The Matrix*, which really does no more than present once again the mental experiment of the "brain in a tank", which was popular twenty years ago, which was in turn an easily recognizable reworking of the myth of the cave, combined with similar arguments presented by Plato in the *Sophist*.

the research sector that has been applied most incisively to manufacturing in the various forms of industrial automation. More broadly, however, the expansion of the Internet is linked to the possibility of performing real actions – buying, selling, learning, going for a walk or having sex – without ever leaving home, simply by arranging symbols on a keyboard and a screen. The consequence has been a dizzying growth in the *performative* function of language – its capacity to *bring about* states of affairs, rather than merely describing them (see Austin 1962).

A quick recapitulation of the concept of *performativity* needs to be made at this point. As is generally known, it was J.L. Austin who gave the term philosophical currency in the early 1960s. He began by observing that, in certain cases, linguistic utterances do not have their usual function of representing, truly or falsely, a state of affairs, but of *performing an action* that "one might not perform, at least not with so much precision, in any other way" (Austin 1962, pp. 271–281), without pronouncing certain words: a promise, for example, or a marriage, or a threat (see Austin 1962, p. 49). Throughout his work Austin insisted that this performative function cannot be limited to a specific class of utterances, but is virtually inscribed in any actual linguistic act. As a result, the social sciences assumed that informatization could bring out this *practical* dimension of words, and the theory of linguistic acts, which derived from the neutral terrain of analytical philosophy, briefly became in the early 1980s the main battlefield of the clash between modern and post-modern, in what may have been the last real moment of speculative vitality in European critical thought. However, even before this application to the sociological field, while the theory was still being discussed by philosophers and linguists, it had already seemed clear that, whatever the importance of the performative in language generally, it has a special connection with certain specific, homogeneous grammatical formulas, such as "I promise that *p*" or "I declare that *p*", although none of these formulas need actually be uttered for the linguistic act to take place (see Benveniste 1963). This is an important aspect, as careful analysis of these particular formulas brings out the logical requisites on which the performative effectiveness of language is actually based, giving us the exemplary illustration we need for an overall view of the forms of communication that define present-day society.

First, we should note that, in these cases, a clear distinction between facts and representations becomes impossible on principle. As Émile Benveniste was the first to note, all the classical performative formulas tend to be *self-referential*, in the sense that the *fact* they refer to is literally *produced* by the representation, as long as it fulfils the socially prescribed requisites. To take some canonical examples: two people are only *genuinely* married if, and only if, the formula "I pronounce you man and wife" is uttered; and if the chairman of a meeting states, "I declare the meeting open", the meeting is *ipso facto* open, nor could it be otherwise.

Second, this coincidence between facts and representations is intimately related to how *power* circulates, both in that it presupposes a socially recognized power, and that it also functions as an ideal tool for reinforcing it. The examples above are already indicative in this sense of a principle that can be extended to all the classic performative formulas: the power of words in themselves can perform an act – celebrate a marriage, sentence a criminal, or declare war – but only if the speaker possesses the *authority* of a priest, a judge, or a sovereign. However, this relation also holds inversely: if someone *successfully* carries out a performative act, whether he has the right to or not – if, for example, he declares war and a war actually breaks out – that person has effectively ratified an actual power in the act of exercising it.

We shall see later what weight this circular relationship between authority and power may have in the specific field of *political* practice. Already, however, it has inevitably pervaded the sphere of general *social* communication since information technology has blurred the distinction between facts and words. We can see this in the *reflexiveness* of all the great communication systems in the present, which, with the instantaneous speed of the new technologies, can communicate on their subject and on themselves *at the same time*, setting up a kind of short circuit whose most obvious expression is provided by so-called "self-fulfilling prophecies". Very summarily, the short circuit is due to the fact that the equilibrium of a communication system must be based on *collective expectations* that fix each time the rules are in force, and which, logically, react to the most reliable information. This means that if you inject an item of information strongly and plausibly enough into the system – for example, that the stock market is about to collapse, or that a certain political party is becoming more popular in the polls – this can influence communication to the point of making something a fact that was originally pure fantasy. It is superfluous to add that the degree of *success* in these cases increases the credibility of the source, only strengthening the circle between authority and power, which had made the success possible at the outset.

The late-modern received wisdom, by which reality and illusion are now indistinguishable and everything is reduced to a simulacrum, is clearly related to this reflexiveness, although it has often offered a vaguely mythological version of it. Unquestionably, however, information technology and reflexiveness tend to stimulate each other, thus changing from within every kind of social institution interested in reinforcing itself, and driving it towards what we might call a *race for the symbolic creation of facts*. The most striking, and at times slightly flamboyant, aspect is that the fundamental rules of the race are, at bottom, the same for every kind of competitor, whether it is a political party or a church, a business or a minority special-interest movement such as the one we have seen at work in the case of multiple personality. For all of them, their prime aim will be to obtain maximum *visibility*, since the overall actual incidence of social communication obviously depends on this. More generally, there will be a tendency to maximize the degree of internal informatization, which means increasing speed and capacity of transmission, while reducing to a minimum the residual materials, the counterweights and constraints that have aspects of reality too static and rigid to adapt to the flow of communication. In a nutshell, we might say that the prime necessity for all of them is *lightness*, though each institution will achieve this in its own specific ways.[3]

3 A "light" political party will replace the rigid and expensive traditional network of sections, bureaucrats and local offices with computerized communication; above all, it will

To assess the importance of this gradual standardization we need to remember that, throughout modern history, the different social sectors have never stopped emphasizing their mutual autonomy, to the point that their diversification into so many independent systems is normally regarded as a sign of the degree of a society's modernization. Now, while this diversification is not formally disappearing – given that the coherence of a religious faith does not guarantee its political success, any more than the scientific truth of a theory determines its commercial value – it is a fact that the shared need for performative effectiveness is creating transversal connections that cross the reciprocal borders and reduce their value. In this way, complex *networks* of chains of communication are taking shape that essentially neutralize the reciprocal autonomy of the various social sectors and are able to connect, for example, a system of scientific research and a religious sect, or a political party and a company, a current of opinion and the marketing strategy of a multinational into a hybrid entity. In particular, in the gradual expansion imposed by the competition between the various social networks, it is inevitable that importance and power gradually shift from the individual nodes of the network, whatever they may be, towards the *connectors* that ensure the stability and expansion of the network. It will be these connectors, without content of their own, and guided by the one formal criterion of maximizing its potential, that dictate the decisions and strategies for the whole system.

4 Micro-worlds

However short and schematic they may be, these brief remarks on late-modern social dynamics should also help us grasp one last aspect of the informatization of the social processes, which is the most significant one for the problems that concern us here.

It is a question, first of all, of recognizing that there is a logical limit to how far we can reduce reality to the circulation of symbols. No symbolic system can handle the infinite variety of contingencies, exceptions and unforeseen events that are virtually included in an actual practical situation. For an operation of data processing to be applied successfully to reality, reality must already have been filtered, domesticated and freed of any possible interference. Virtually, one can computerize *even* these operations, which precede the real action and that outline what in technical jargon is called its frame. However, each of these preliminary operations would require its own frame in turn, and so further actions of cleaning and domesticating the environment, and so on. In the end, the performativity of

tend to reduce its ties with a class, a social grouping or a precise social category, so as to address a non-specific public of ordinary people. The "lighter" a commercial business is, the more its profits will depend on the simple impact of its "logo", the message connected with its brand, and its "philosophy", while the activities of material production are reduced to an insignificant detail, governed by the one criterion of reducing costs to a minimum. On this question in general, see Boltanski and Chiapello (2000).

the *symbolic* operations should in any case presuppose *real* actions of control that guarantee their frame.

In the early 1970s, to solve what was then called the "frame problem", the pioneers of artificial intelligence coined a particularly striking technical term: *micro-world*.[4] A traditional robot, programmed for industrial purposes, for example, may successfully operate only in its own specific micro-world: that is to say, in a logical space that is rigidly marked out, from which any kind of unforeseen contingency has already been rigorously eliminated, apart from the more or less numerous variants envisaged by the program.

At the time, it was still seriously thought possible to extend and connect the micro-worlds of a conventional machine, to the point of reproducing the openness to the world typical of human intelligence. In the course of time, this has proved to be an unsustainable epistemological naivety. In our mental operations contingency and the unforeseen are not the result of a quantitative accumulation of complexity; on the contrary, any attempt to mark out a circumscribed field of clear rules and expectations must, first of all, accept an undifferentiated openness to the possible, in which *anything* might prove to be significant, and contingency, on principle, *has no limits*. In short, the *world* of the human mind is not a simple total of micro-worlds, and the previous chapters have already given us an idea of how much the problem of unlimited contingency impacts on every action of establishing a psychic identity.

The *social* dynamic, however, is different from the psychic one, particularly once information technology has gradually stripped down the content to the advantage of the purely formal criteria that expand and strengthen the network. This will eliminate any internal resistance to a remodelling of the whole dynamic of communication in the direction that best suits the information processes. Taking just the slightest terminological liberty, we can therefore say that the greater the level of informatization in a social network, the more *it will tend to generate its own micro-world*, from which contingencies and exceptions beyond a certain limit must be excluded to avoid paralyzing the system. *Two* kinds of heterogeneous but interdependent operations are therefore combined in the processes of social reproduction: *symbolic* operations inside the micro-world, but which have no material connotation; and *real* operations of control, security and elimination of contingency, which ensure the stability of the micro-world.

The internal connections of a social network will always naturally tend to reinforce themselves, and in principle there is no limit to this expansion: a call centre in Asia may be connected to a phone company in Europe, which may give its logo to a holiday village in the Caribbean, and all of them may belong to a religious sect supporting a conservative leader in America. The more extensive the network,

4 Various authors, the most famous of whom were perhaps Minsky and Winograd, used the term "micro-world". For a clear critical account of the logical problems connected with this concept, see Dreyfus (1981). On the frame problem, see also Dennett (1990).

however, the stronger the need to deliver it from the unpredictability of the world, tracing a clear boundary between inner and outer, a protective barrier between symbols and real bodies. The micro-world in which the symbolic operations take place and where we are therefore invited to communicate and interact each time, will tend to be wholly *anaesthetized* to guarantee the fluidity of the symbols (see Montani 2007). The *outside* world, by contrast, is seen as anonymous disorder, a threat, in which anything can happen and any unforeseen occurrence, however slight, can cause a catastrophe in the communication flow.[5]

At this point it is difficult to ignore the fact that the social construction of a micro-world presents various striking analogies with the mechanism of dissociation. In both cases, the real is perceived essentially as a destructive threat; in both, the desire for protection erects a wall between inside and outside, severing the links between the two regions: and finally, in both, this defensive strategy is situated in the grey area where facts and representations become indistinguishable. To grasp the true sense of this analogy, however, we must be careful not to banally place the social and the psychic on the same level. On the contrary, if the social systems are driven in this direction, it is precisely because *they do not obey any psychology*, but entrust their reproduction, with blind linearity, to the criterion of maximizing their potential. On the other hand, from the point of view of individuals and their psychic equilibrium, a micro-world clearly has all the requisites to become a perfect "psychic retreat", and it is natural for the social networks to encourage this kind of reception, as its roots in individual psychology are an indispensable ingredient for its performative effectiveness. In this way, the joint pressure of psychic and social needs forms a curious *late-modern social pact*, in which a desire to belong to one communication network or another, and to settle psychologically in one micro-world or another, protects individuals from the looming annihilation anxiety in the outside world, and ensures the chosen network greater power than its potential competitors.

We shall have the opportunity later to consider the implications of this pact on the specifically *political* terrain. Meanwhile, however, this first schematic description will help us define more precisely the concept that has been our underlying theme so far. The term *niche*, then, signifies the partial or total overlapping between the need to mark out a micro-world imposed by highly computerized social networks, and the need to protect oneself from unlimited contingency felt by a psychic system that feels its existence threatened by exposure to the world. A niche in this sense is a space that is partly real and partly symbolic, the result of the *interpenetration* of social and psychic operations. However, if our theory is true, it will not be one space among others, but the *basic* dimension in

5 It should be added that one can communicate on this possible catastrophe, thus reintroducing it into the power mechanisms internal to the social networks, but without reducing its threatening nature. The collusion between the creators of viruses and companies producing antiviruses is a less dramatic example of this, but just as eloquent as the link between terrorist groups and sovereign states.

which, in the present-day world, this interpenetration takes place. In other words, wherever the social networks combine with the needs and drives of individual minds, a niche will tend to be created with its specific confines, its order, its inner tensions, and the passages that connect it with the outside world.

5 The game and its rules

If we now return to our previous distinction between successful and unsuccessful dissociation, it is not easy to decide in which of the two categories this particular dialectic between niches and micro-worlds should go. On the one hand, our scheme involves constructive cooperation between psychic mechanisms and social dynamics, and, in this sense, we can certainly say that the dissociation is *successful*, in that it is functional and adaptive to the needs imposed by the communication processes. On the other hand, the cooperation between psychic and social demands does not seem to be seeking to master external reality at all, but to *deny* it, in a form that therefore recalls the pathological element in dissociation rather than the functional and constructive one. As an uncontrollable source of noise, the outside world is essentially seen as a threat, and the appeal of social networks for individuals is the desire to defend themselves from it.

Examining this aspect we shall be able to understand how much this link remains ambiguous, complex and, in the end, more fragile than it might appear at first sight. In a niche, the social and psychic dimensions are superimposed, confused and bound one to another, but *they do not actually coincide*, nor could they ever, on principle. We should not forget that in the psychic economy of our species, relation to unlimited contingency has a structural value, even though this openness may come into conflict with a need for protection that is no less profound. The core of the anthropological paradox consists precisely in the fact that it is from openness to unlimited contingency that the two basic aspects of the symbolic faculty – language and praxis – draw the capacity and the onus to make the distinction between signal and noise each time, starting from their indistinctness. In this way, they can *also* satisfy the demand for protection in a form that seems to be inaccessible to any other living species.

By contrast, a micro-world is defined precisely by *excluding* openness of this kind. Logically, then, not only the psychology, but, more generally, the *humanity* of the subjects that act and communicate is a virtual source of disturbance in it that undermines from *within* the regular fluidity of symbols and the ascetic coherence by which the social network always seeks only to maximize its potential. The term *micro-world* should remind us, in short, that a highly computerized social mechanism will naturally transform the world into a kind of *second-level animal environment*, a "second nature" in which the social rules acquire the same obligatory status as instincts and signals, "optimize" the flow of communication, separating signal and noise *once and for all.* This demand for order, however, clashes with the ineradicable "noise" that is already implicit in the psychic existence of subjects and makes it impossible to reduce praxis and language to behaviour and instinctual signals.

The crucial point is that in a computerized economy, the primary resource for reproducing and increasing a social network's power is no longer physical labour in the strict sense, but the symbolic faculty – the general human capacity to innovate productive processes, reshape communication, and combine and change the rules in completely unpredictable ways, starting from the unlimited contingency of the indistinctness between signal and noise. In other words, the general *creativity* of the human animal is, for every micro-world, at the same time the most important resource and the most important threat. Conversely, the frame surrounding the micro-world is, for individual subjects, a precious source of protection and security, but also a limitation, an artificial barrier that is extraneous and oppressive.

Nothing better illustrates this contradiction than the ambivalence in data processing of the logical *play* space – the prototype, as we know, of creative activity, and therefore of successful dissociation. As is generally known, information technology has meant that any productive activity resembles the model of a game with rules. Whether that activity is developing a scientific theory, preparing a marketing strategy or launching bombs on civilians, in every case the crucial resource will be mastery of the rules of the game, speed in innovation, and the creativity with which these rules can be bent to an unforeseen and original performance. However, it is inevitable that this creative faculty is virtually open to the *denial* or reformulation of existing rules, and to that kind of unlimited contingency that Wittgenstein expressed so incisively: "The first thought, in setting up an ethical law of the form 'thou shalt…' is: And what if I do not do it?" (Wittgenstein 1921, 6.422). Paradoxically situated both inside and outside the logical space of the game, a *human* player always has relative sovereignty over the rules. This may induce him to enter and leave various social networks and opportunistically exploit their competitiveness, circumvent their rules and confines, and, in a word, *dissociate himself* from the micro-world that claims to protect him, to the point of seriously endangering its delicate internal equilibrium.

It is clear, in short, that while all may seem more or less at peace on the surface of a niche, there will always be a field of tensions below the surface and a potential battlefield between its poles. This terrain we are in is scarred with conflicts, and the emergence of creativity does nothing to allay it, but merely marks the front line.

Chapter 4

Different ways of building a world

In the beginning all the World was America.

John Locke, *Two Treatises of Government*

1 Conventions and rituality

In the previous chapter, we tried to understand how social and psychic dynamics interact with and condition each other in the late-modern world under the driving force of technological innovation, particularly information technology in communications. The basic conjecture was that diverse social institutions and practices tend to combine in complex networks; that these networks tend to stabilize, generating each time a *micro-world*; and that, as a rule, this structure relies on the dissociative attitudes of individuals, giving the mechanisms of ego-splitting a constructive function that is the antithesis of the classical modern idea of subjectivity.

It also seemed clear that, as this tangle of social and psychic dynamics is ambiguous at its heart, it is subject to striking fluctuations. On the one hand, micro-worlds offer individuals a retreat from unlimited contingency, responding to a demand for protection that has become more and more acute with the crisis in the socio-political equilibrium of the past. On the other, to optimize their internal dynamics and development, they have to adopt rigorous mechanisms of inclusion/exclusion, which, by definition, exclude the moments of openness to contingency, which are essential for the symbolic faculty to express itself authentically and happily. Individuals, in turn, respond to this ambivalence of the social systems in a way that reflects the intimate bipolarity of the dissociative mechanisms, wavering between a fetishistic adherence to the micro-world, which amounts to denying external reality, and an opportunistic betrayal of any local system of rules, which mirrors a dissociation that affects the whole of the social sphere.

It is almost superfluous to add that this is no more than a general, abstract account, as well as being purely hypothetical. Mention of the dual ambivalence of its polarities, however, in itself suggests how many different variants there may be that are compatible with this general scheme. We need, then, to consider it empirically, to establish whether it really applies to the forms of life in the present, and, if so, to learn to distinguish the various actual figures, the tensions, the risks and the developing opportunities that are implicit in this dialectic between niches and micro-worlds. However, before doing this, we might wonder how far and under what conditions this theory really manages to reconcile the two intertwined aspects of the idea of an ontology of the present: that of "now only" and that of "always". Granted, from the start we have superimposed on the description of specifically contemporary phenomena and problems explicit reference to the general constitution of human beings, whose basic characteristic lies in what I have called the "anthropological paradox". So far, however, this superimposition has been more a matter of principle than the coherent upshot of a consideration of the facts. We still need to verify whether an entwining of the psychic and social planes, so typically contemporary and so dependent on recent historical factors such as the new technologies, can really claim "ontological" value and give us, however indirectly, a prospect onto the human condition in general.

Such an abrupt jump in the argument, from the plane of the present-day world to the generally anthropological one, logically requires a decisive broadening of perspective and recourse to interpretative tools unlike those deployed so far. Fortunately, our first steps can follow a well-trodden path, as the humanities have shown increasing interest in a topic that was central to the previous chapter – the *performativeness of communication acts.*

I have already noted that the question of the performative, which Austin discovered and developed on the terrain of general philosophy, enjoyed unexpected popularity in the late 1970s in research specifically designed for understanding *contemporary* society (see Lyotard 1979, Habermas 1981). Almost at the same time, another original line of thought took shape that developed the questions launched by Austin in the specific sphere of anthropology, particularly in studies intended to interpret *ritual practices* (see Tambiah 1985, Turner 1986, Rappaport 1999). To understand the reasoning behind this second line of research, we need only recall that the performative effectiveness of words is clearly not an invention of modern information technology, but a correlate of human language in general. Every known human society has systematically used this potentiality to confer on certain formulas, uttered in the right circumstances, the power of *immediately* bringing about such important events as a marriage, a solemn undertaking, or a war. If we consider its effectiveness in the abstract, this fusion of words and facts seems almost magic in its power, and it may well be that this similarity is worth considering. Indeed, anthropologists advanced the theory some time ago that this performative function of language may be at the origin of magic beliefs in the creative power of the word.[1] In any case, the power of performative formulas certainly has severer limits than those attributed to magic: it can turn a peasant into a knight, but not water into wine; it can make a promise real, but cannot guarantee that the promise will actually be honoured. The first task of an anthropology of performativeness, then, will be to trace in general terms the confines of this grey area, in which representation is effectively *equivalent to* reality.

1 See Rappaport (1999, p. 126) and, more generally, Rosier-Catach (2004).

In trying to answer this question, Austin had insisted on the *conventional* nature of performative acts, adding that "it is difficult to say where conventions begin and end" (Austin 1962, p. 118). It is true, in fact, that only *institutional* events can be made real by a simple performative formula, as they alone are completely governed by convention. According to Austin, however, even in these cases we cannot completely separate the conventions from the facts, or, in his terminology, the *illocutionary* and *perlocutionary* moments of the speech act. What happens if the president declares the meeting open and no one listens? If a marriage, a baptism, or a trial is celebrated following all the rules, but is received with a shrug and, to all intents and purposes, *does not come into force*? As we can see, invoking a rule or a pact that has been established once and for all is not enough to guarantee that the conventions take effect, unless there is also a shared understanding, here and now, by those joining in the game, who can give substance to the conventional order, reassuring each of them that the others are committed to playing the game too.

Unlike "conventions" in the usual sense, this understanding must be an actual existential reality, and not just an agreement worked out at the drawing-board. Rather, it needs to be an agreement between the *forms of life*, a sharing of habits and expectations that is sufficient to fix the *normality* on which the actual norms rest.[2] Once again, though: how does one reach agreement on *how* "normality" is in force in the very act of applying a norm? How does one prevent the conventional order from dissolving in daily use, rather than controlling and reducing its complexity? In response to these difficulties, since the pre-history of humanity cultural evolution has selected a particular type of practice: that of *ritual*, which defines the mutual interchange between convention and institution, so as to reduce their internal fragility to a minimum.

In effect, the affinity between ritual practices and performative speech acts has been noted since the first discussions between philosophers, linguists and anthropologists on the questions raised by Austin, if only for the obvious fact that the canonical examples of performatives – a promise, a baptism, or a judicial sentence – all come without exception from the sphere of ritual. There is, however, a crucial operation in a genuine rite that has now disappeared in merely conventional acts, or survives in it only marginally. To be as succinct as possible, we might say that ritual is orchestrated so as to fuse two dimensions: that of present, contingent reality and that of a cosmic order that is unvarying and therefore indisputable. Ratifying a performative act – a wedding, a coronation or a vow – with a rite means, in short, binding present contingency to the unvarying cosmic order, making the conventions adopted *sacred*, and therefore beyond discussion. In this way, ritual practice does much more than bring about something performatively by appealing to a convention: at bottom, it creates the preliminary conditions by which a society *can give itself binding conventions at all*. In other words,

2 As is generally known, the subject is treated in exemplary fashion by Wittgenstein (1947). We shall see shortly, however, that the connections between norms and normality are decisive in the conception of the politician proposed by Schmitt (1932).

"performativeness itself may be made possible by ritual" (Rappaport 1999, p. 118): taking part in a rite means implicitly accepting a certain liturgical order and, therefore, *being obliged*, publicly and incontrovertibly, to respect all the collective norms contained in it. In practice, nothing can guarantee that this commitment will actually be maintained in future. However, whether it is confirmed or betrayed, the collective obligation is still witnessed by the rite and, in any case, ensures the primary level of a "social contract", the *normality* on which norms and conventions rest (Rappaport 1999, pp. 137–138).

Here we should not forget that, in the view of all the major authorities, what ritual provides is not *one* solution among many, but a primary anthropological structure, without alternatives or functional equivalents. This is supported in the first place by the empirical fact of the existence of ritual in practically every known human culture. Of course, the particular rites differ vastly in each culture, and dozens of them may exist in the same society with completely different modalities and functions. However, not only do these practices display striking family resemblances, but the affinity becomes still more marked, the more we study some of the formal characteristics that define rituality as such, so there is nothing extravagant in speculating that *ritual form* may count as an anthropological universal (see Rappaport 1999). We might add that this formal universality is particularly marked in what is unquestionably the heart of specifically human rituality – *religious* ritual. Indeed, one of the major authorities in classical antiquity has recently conjectured that religion should be regarded as "a long-lived hybrid between the cultural and the biological tradition" (Burkert 1998, p. 20). A further aspect of this biological root of human rituality is its significant analogy with *ritualization* practices that are widespread in the animal world.[3]

To avoid misunderstanding, I am not offering a "reductionist" reading of ritual practices, which is in any case widely contradicted by the empirical evidence. It is indisputable that religious ritual is an exclusively human trait, and that in no other species is there anything that can be compared to the "sacred" or the "divine". The point is that it is ritual practice itself that in many exemplary cases involves something similar to a cultural performance of animality, for example emphasizing the "indexical" value in symbols, which they share with animal signals, or forcing the actions to "mimic" instinctive behaviours. In short, everything suggests that

3 In ethology, "ritualization" indicates the particular phylogenetic transformation of an innate instinctive module in such a way that the original specific function of that behaviour is gradually replaced by a purely *communicative* function. For example, a module of combat is performed to no purpose, with the aim of *signalling* a disposition to fight; or the movements connected with the preparation of the nest are "displayed" by the male for the purposes of courtship, and so on. The most significant aspect is that, in this process, formalisms, stereotypes and superfluousness are emphasized in the behaviour to the point of *mimic exaggeration* (Lorenz 1999), the clear sense being to make the signal being transmitted *unequivocal*. Hence, the logical deduction that, in general, animal behaviour tends to be ritualized in cases where any *misunderstanding* could have disastrous consequences, to the point that the transparency of the signal becomes the primary biological purpose (Schechner 1987).

the power of ritual is linked to its capacity to exhibit the *threshold* of anthropogenesis, placing itself in that border area between the symbolic and sub-symbolic, where dissociative practices, too, are rooted. For our purposes, it is therefore highly significant that, as we shall see now, the ritual space displays *all the structural features of a "successful" and socially constructive dissociation*. To clarify this aspect, however, we shall need to focus more clearly, at least in their general lines, on the actual techniques and modalities with which ritual practice – when it succeeds – neutralizes the paradox of conventionality inherent in institutional practices.

2 Ritual as exception and paradigm

First, let us consider that to perform its sacral function of linking the contingent and cosmic dimensions, ritual must necessarily be sharply distinguished from profane practices, which refer only to present reality. The ritual space therefore needs to be *isolated* inside a clearly defined perimeter, given *exceptional* attributes, and any functional connection it may have with the rest of the collective life suspended. In a recent study Catherine Bell has called this work of separation and distinction *ritualization*, suggesting very convincingly that the basic (and perhaps anthropologically universal) moment in ritual should be sought, not so much in its content, but in precisely this need to fix a boundary and mark a difference.[4] On the other hand, a rite certainly cannot be *only* a distinct space, separated from the profane one, if it must ensure a stable foundation for conventions and set up in practice the normality on which collective norms rest. To this end, a rite must be able to constitute a *model*, or, more exactly, a *paradigm*, for ordinary practices: something that is literally *beside* (*parà*) them and therefore remains *separate*, while still dictating the *exemplary* forms.

This need to function as both *exception* and *paradigm*, being separate from reality so as to control it, lays ritual open to a logical difficulty not unlike that facing infant play. Although the cosmic order evoked by the liturgy is offered as absolute and unquestionable, at bottom it can only be a *convention*, since there is no order to which human beings are bound by any logical or biological necessity. *Communicating* the liturgical order thus already involves the risk of displaying its conventionality, revealing the incontrovertible truth that everything that can be *said* can equally be *negated*. The procedure has to be *ritualized*, precisely so as to break this circle, which risks paralyzing action in unlimited contingency. The specific performance of ritual, in other words, consists in *negating* this contingency, in

4 See Bell (1992, p. 74): "I will use the term 'ritualization' to draw attention to the way in which certain social actions strategically distinguish themselves in relation to other actions. In a very preliminary sense, ritualization is a way of acting that is designed and orchestrated to distinguish and privilege what is being done in relation to other, usually more quotidian, activities. As such, ritualization is a matter of various culturally specific activities, for [...] creating and privileging a qualitative distinction between the 'sacred' and the 'profane' [...]"

conferring on the liturgical order a binding necessity – making its principles count as *tautologies* that cannot be denied.

It is well known that in religious systems, many different ingredients are involved in this function: from the effectively quasi-tautological character of the supreme liturgical formulas ("there is no god but God", "being is and non-being is not"), to all the habits and mythologems in every religion that help make an arbitrary system of beliefs seem obvious. *This order*, with its definitions and details, has to be transfigured into *Order* as such, without alternatives, and only a ritual practice in the strict sense can perform this task, because it is in the closed perimeter of ritual that the liturgical order can stand as exemplary. It is here that the *absolute negation* of disorder, contingency and the chaos inherent in the human condition is publicly acted out. If, however, we try to decipher the actual form that this negation acquires in ritual procedure, we will find a paradox that has always struck and fascinated modern observers. Surprisingly, what occupies the centre of the ritual scene is usually *the exact opposite of any possible order* – unlimited contingency, the indistinct and nothingness.

Since the earliest systematic research in anthropology, it has been noted that, though ritual's explicit function is to stabilize the social order, frequently, if not invariably, this order is *suspended* in the circumscribed space of the rite, along with the hierarchies and rules that are supposed to have this stabilizing effect. At the same time, disorder, formlessness and chaos are often evoked and unleashed with such force that an impartial observer such as Radcliffe-Brown conjectured that "creat[ing] a sense of insecurity" was the most authentic aim of ritual. Certainly, the chaotic element is always rigorously confined to precise times and places, and, if order is suspended in the "liminal" phase of the celebration, it is only so as to re-establish it more powerfully in the final phase. The function of order in ritual is not being denied or contradicted, then. Nevertheless, theories like Turner's *anti-structure* or De Martino's *cultural apocalypses*, which extend this dynamic between order and disorder to ritual form as such, raise an inescapable question: if the point is the negation of disorder, why is there such an open emphasis on the *negative* of this negation? Why, in the anthropologically *basic* form of its social life, does the supposed "world-former" seem to insist on staging the opposite of any form, on exorcizing and evoking, on provoking and containing chaos, rather than promptly eliminating it?

The most convincing response is that it is precisely this shift of emphasis onto the negative that ensures that ritual has the value of a *paradigm*. What every rule, every order and every form have in common is their opposing unlimited contingency, formlessness and chaos. So, the more a specific representation seems *correlated* with formlessness, as its obverse or negation, the more it will appear *exemplary* of any possible "form" in general – and, therefore, the expression of the *absolute* order of things, without alternatives or possibilities of negation that are not Nothingness as such. Logically, this, too, is a construction that can only take place in an exceptional symbolic space *dissociated* from ordinary reality. What a community *actually* has to confront will each time be a specific problem: *this* epidemic, *this* external enemy, or *this* crisis in the balance of power. There is never, in short, an experience of disorder or chaos *in themselves* until the symbolic order of a rite envelops this or that contingent threat and sees there the manifestation of an indistinct power, which requires an exemplary act of negation in response. Thanks to this complex structure, ritual manages to be *both an exception and a paradigm*, thus following the pattern of *successful* dissociation.

In conclusion, the space set up by ritual proves to be extraordinarily complex. On the one hand, as we have seen, it is a closed dimension that has been carefully separated from the outside world. At the same time, though, as in Borges's myth of the Aleph, this kind of niche is like a window onto the indefinite, which *includes* within itself unlimited contingency. It is needless to add that this construct will avail itself unconditionally of the dissociative potential of the psyche: mystical and religious traditions provide almost unlimited case histories in the matter. Had we time to go through them all, we might note that even in the most extreme cases, as long as the sacred/profane dichotomy is the one structuring collective life, it will be the *social* codes, rather than individual psychic discretion, that mark when and how one may legitimately cross the symbolic confines.

What is essential is that, overall, this correlation between the psychic and social planes should correspond precisely to the challenge of the anthropological paradox, taking us straight to the core of this paradox – the ambivalence of openness to the world, which is specific to the human animal. As will be recalled, it has seemed inevitable from the start that the concept of "world", which in this sense is typically anthropological, has to indicate *both* the delimited and coherent symbolic space in which a specific culture exists, *and* the unlimited infinity of external contingencies, against which this code erects a barrier. Now, thanks to a symbolic structure that fuses the limit with the unlimited, the ritual space is able to neutralize this paradoxical duality, satisfying at once the two contrasting requirements of *openness* and *protection*. As they are directly exposed to the power of the negative, each participant in the rite is freed of any constraint and cultural inhibition, literally called upon to *inaugurate from nothing* the conventions that regulate the collective life. However, as it takes place in a delimited space, in which every move is prescribed by an unvarying ceremony, this inaugural act will inevitably tend to *reproduce* an order that is in force "now and forever", in which contingency is therefore absorbed and neutralized.

In his preparatory studies for his unfinished essay on "cultural apocalypses", Ernesto De Martino had clearly intuited how profoundly exemplary the ancient Roman ritual of the *mundus* was in this connection. In it the complexity of openness to the *world* was literally staged, expressing with extraordinary clarity the inner dynamic and the function of rituality in general (see De Martino 1977, pp. 212–217). The *mundus* was the name of a circular ditch of two storeys, situated in the centre of "*Roma quadrata*", the supposed original enclosure of the city. According to the myth, when the city was founded, the first citizens each threw into this ditch a clod of earth from their own area of origin, covering the first fruits that Romulus had offered in sacrifice. The lower storey of the *mundus* was consecrated to Ceres, and so to the earth, but was also connected with the underworld, the cult of the Manes and the world of the dead, while the upper storey was connected with the dimension of the "*superi*" – the inhabited world and the heavenly sphere. So, in the *mundus* an "above" and a "below" of cosmic dimensions met, which therefore literally projected the unlimited extension of the *world* into the limited space of ritual.

The ditch was ritually opened on three days only, indicated in the calendars as *comitiales*. On these days, on which *mundus patet*, all normal administrative activity was suspended, apart from the most urgent business: there was neither combat nor speech-making, no ship weighed anchor, and no soldier was enlisted. The dead returned to wander the earth, chaos reigned in the city, and every boundary between high and low was dissolved, until the closing of the ditch ritually repeated the foundation of Rome, giving it a cosmic value of absolute negation of chaos and, quite literally, *the foundation of the world*.

In his grand project, which was abruptly cut short by his death, De Martino intended to reconstruct this dialectic, which includes in the world the threat of its dissolution, as it is found in the most varied cultural and religious traditions. He used psychopathological case histories as his touchstone, not least the symptoms of derealization and depersonalization, which are now usually connected with dissociative phenomena. Logically, the link between collective practice, conveyed by socially shared symbols, and an intrapsychic dynamic inseparable from individual experience, is a delicate and equivocal area of research, particularly if one intends to make it into a general anthropological conception. However, with all the required caution, we may reasonably draw at least two general conclusions from the range of phenomena we have glanced at in these pages. First, thanks to its dual connotation – as both *paradigm* and *exception* – ritual practices are no mere denial of reality with illusions, or the erection of a symbolic retreat from the outside world, or the creation of a simple artificial niche that can, at best, compensate for the supposed shortcomings of an environment that is genetically prescribed for the human animal. They can, quite literally, *open a world*, in all the complex senses of the term that Heidegger tried to bring out. Second, this cultural goal could only be achieved by regularly attending a socially prescribed space *dissociated* from ordinary reality, in which symbols and facts are inextricably fused.

3 The sovereignty of the moderns

These remarks clarify what has been one of our implicit premises from the start: that only with the advent of *modern* society has dissociative behaviour lost all its constructive value and been labelled as pathological or indicative of a failure to constitute a subjectivity, which is a process now firmly based on repressing the drives and submitting to the law. In particular, we can now start to intuit why this new view of the psychic mechanisms has coincided with a broader historical process, one designed to gradually loosen the social institutions from their ritual and religious shell.

This specific feature of the process of modernization, in which what was once sanctified by ritual is now re-consigned to the everyday world, has for some time been designated in German culture with the term *Verweltlichung* – literally "*mundanization*". Today, however, the same subject is usually referred to by the term "*secularization*", a concept originating in canon law, from which it migrated to juridical science and theology (see Marramao 1994). If we had time to follow its progress, this simple alternation of terms might already give us two significant clues. First, as the symbolic strategy orchestrated by ritual gradually declined, the task of *instituting the world* was completely redefined, taken from the hands of priests and given to navigators and cartographers (see Sloterdijk 1999), and, in this transition from the symbolic to the real, it took on an inner opacity that still weighs on Heidegger's attempts to radically rethink openness to the world as a correlate of man's humanity. Second, the fact that a term of juridical-ecclesiastical origin has prevailed, demonstrates just how far secularization has remained an ambivalent process, which has been able to free modern institutions of their religious foundation only by maintaining the logic, concepts and functions of that lost foundation, reproducing them *in* the new institutional systems.

The lines of this complex and ambivalent dynamic are still subject to constant historiographic revision, and here we can only consider one aspect, taken from a text that specifically discusses the ambivalence of secularization, Carl Schmitt's *Political Theology*.[5] As is generally known, this work has become a classic of political theory, above all for its skill in defining the most important and ambivalent of modern political concepts, that of *sovereignty*, with a simple, concise formula: "sovereign is he who decides on the exception" (Schmitt 1922, p. 2). What concerns us here, however, is that in illustrating at length the status and prerogatives of the sovereign, Schmitt seems to attribute to him exactly the function that was once transferred to ritual practice.

In effect, the system of norms, injunctions and sentences that structures the modern legal system cannot escape the circularity that, for the logical reasons we have already mentioned, threatens the performative effectiveness of any conventional order. Legality too, overall, needs *legitimizing*, and it is illusory to think that the juridical order might rest in turn *on a norm* (Schmitt 1922, p. 16). In realistic terms, the problem is that "every general norm demands a normal, everyday frame of life", because "there exists no norm that is applicable to chaos" (ibid., p. 13). We therefore need to "create the situation in which legal norms may be effective" (ibid.), "a normal situation must exist", and this, according to Schmitt, is what the sovereign can perform: "the sovereign produces and guarantees the situation in its totality" (ibid.).

We already know that a similar "normal, everyday frame of life" in traditional societies was the first fruit of ritual systems. However, we should not expect to

5 The references to Schmitt in this chapter and the next will inevitably be circumscribed to some specific problems. For a complete picture of Schmitt's work and its internal development, see Galli (1996).

find in the acts of a modern sovereign anything similar to the systematic refinement of the drives, the harmonization of collective behaviour, and the institution of a unified symbolic code, in the way in which the ritualization of procedures constructed normality in archaic societies. Now, according to Schmitt at least, the "creation" of the sovereign is concentrated in a single option: in deciding if the state of normality presumed by the norms actually exists or not: "he is sovereign who definitely decides whether this normal situation actually exists" (Schmitt 1922, p. 13).

In short, the sovereign's function is concentrated and isolated in *one single* basic decision: we might call it an *arch-decision*, as it is logically *distinct* from the thousand decisions that, day by day, make up the actual government of life, and yet he can never lose his authority over this government, as he must constantly ensure its foundation. This dialectic of separation and dominion, a genuine prototype of the "horizontal split" on which modernity stands, is most fully expressed in the sovereign's specific prerogative: that of *declaring a state of exception*. Logically, this declaration is the equivalent of deciding that the state of normality is not present or is under threat to the point of requiring the "suspension of the legal order in its totality" (ibid.) as an extreme defensive measure. With an explicit paradox, in short, "in the case of exception, the state suspends the law by virtue, one might say, of a law of self-preservation" (ibid.). In other words, order is affirmed in the act of suspending it, mirroring the dialectic activated in ritual procedures.

As Schmitt sees it, then, the intrinsic ambivalence of secularization reproduces the requisites of the machinery of ritual within modern political institutions, but reorganizing them in a profoundly changed structure. It would therefore be a complete misunderstanding to think that Schmitt is seeking to minimize the difference between the modern organization of society and the ancient one. On the contrary, the difference is basic, and its *first* expression lies in the fact that while the archaic order was founded, as we have seen, on the *symbolic inclusion* of absolute negativity, the equilibrium instituted by the sovereign requires its *actual exclusion*.

The sovereign's first task, in fact, is that of "ensuring *within* the State and its territory a stable peace, of establishing calm, security and order" (Schmitt 1932, p. 46) because, logically, this is "the premise that gives legal norms their strength" (ibid.). This requires keeping at bay any external enemies, who should be driven back beyond their borders, as well as potential internal enemies, who should be physically expelled, eliminated, exiled, and "expelled from the community of peace" (ibid., p. 47). It is here that we can measure the success of the classical European state, that actually achieved "something most improbable: creating internal peace and eliminating enmity as a legal concept" (ibid., p. 10).

Nothing expresses the profound meaning of this "elimination of enmity" better than Hobbes's conception of the *state of nature*. As is generally known, for Hobbes the first prerogative of the Leviathan is precisely that of rejecting a state of nature where each man is a threat and potential predator to his fellows. However, *pace* the popular view of Hobbes, what generated this virtual "war of all against all" was not a hypothetical aggressive instinct of animal nature, but the specifically human right to question *any* order or principle, against a background of unlimited contingency that authorizes each of the contenders to regard himself as "good, fair and right" (Schmitt 1932, p. 65). Never so much as in Hobbes, then, has openness to *unlimited* contingency been recognized as intrinsic to the *nature* of the human animal. When, however, this natural power is stripped of the robes of sacrality in which ritual dressed it, it appears more as a *threat*. The threat is that of an enemy that the joint force of the citizenry can remove but never wholly eliminate, remaining a permanent focus of the demand for protection: the justified "fear … of violent death", which forces the individual to submit to the sovereign, and is thus the only true *natural* foundation of law and order.

So, what the sovereign guarantees before everything else is the *exclusion* of unlimited contingency from civil life. That is why even a state of exception "is different from anarchy or chaos" (Schmitt 1922, p. 12): because, unlike ritual, its function is not to unleash contingency in a protected, limited space, but just the opposite – to *prevent* this unleashing, to set an extreme barrier, and so preserve order and the rules, even when they are suspended.[6] Thanks to this complex structure, the formal universality of laws can instantly dissolve the circularity that ritual had to undergo each time: a legitimate sovereign makes the current order *ipso facto* the *only* possible order. Its only alternative is the disintegration of the institutions and regression to a state of nature, where there is no limit to contingency and *everything* becomes *possible* again.

4 Symbolic borders and real borders

Let us try to recapitulate the various ideas that have piled up in these last few pages. First, we have found the basic features of *successful* dissociation – those that had already emerged in the dynamics of play, and then in the consequences of computerization – in an archaic form of social life of unchallengeable primary anthropological importance: ritual procedures. In particular, we have found what seemed on the surface to be the most irrational feature of the dissociative mechanism: the tendency to isolate and privilege a space designed to *negate* reality, and yet still *remaining part of it*. Not only did this strategy of negation serve in *mastering* reality, like the other cases of successful dissociation we have discussed, but it was shared by the whole social community in the ancient world, and proved an effective way out of the latent paradox of openness to the world and, thus, of *the human condition in general*. Satisfying the demand for protection as much as that of openness, harmonizing the limited space of the rules and the unlimited space of contingency, is a task that weighs on *any* form of human life, as every

6 Benjamin (1940) appeals to this fact to contrast the state of exception as staged by decree of the dominant power with an "effective state of emergency" that the revolutionary classes would have the task of creating. As we can see, the project is to overturn the political sense of Schmitt's theory while maintaining its basic premises.

human life is open to the world, and "world" is, inevitably, both the unlimited and the limit, both contingency and its negation.

Logically, these few fragmentary hints are mere suggestions that it would be misleading and extravagant to try to turn into something even approaching a scientific theory. My only aim is to verify whether the dialectic between niches and micro-worlds, though it is an exclusively contemporary phenomenon, may not in certain conditions open the way to ontology or, at least, raise legitimate doubts about the anthropological model that has come down to us in modern European culture. However, even this would be beyond our grasp, if we could not plausibly suggest that the logical structure of the "world" itself, as we have reconstructed it, is still at work *even* in modern *Verweltlichung*, in the farewell to rituality and in the overall transformation that has brought about the modern world, making the *horizontal* split between top and bottom the pillar of the social order, as well as of psychic normality.

Following Schmitt's reconstruction, we have conjectured that the first vector of this transformation was the isolating of the sovereign's function in relation to the complex texture of social relations for which the sovereign guarantees "law and order". Schmitt is masterly in demonstrating to what point this distinction between kingdom and government, politics and society, state and civil society, has contributed to ensuring the European nations a long, unchallenged supremacy over other regions of the earth. It remains less clear, however, what *conditions* made the change possible and later dictated to the new order how it would develop internally. From this point of view, the very split between sovereignty and government seems to have generated an illusion, which is palpable in Schmitt, as, at bottom, in many of the studies that take a juridical approach. This split, which is a *result* of the modern order and its way of representing itself, was taken as an actual premise, almost as if the actual social systems, the forms of life, and the concrete modalities of administering power contributed only marginally to the stability of the legal order. By contrast, the line of research initiated by Michel Foucault has only just begun to throw some light on the complex procedures, techniques of government, and systems of exclusion/inclusion, discipline and control, that made it possible for several centuries to have the social machine hinging on such unstable and opaque concepts as "sovereignty", "nation" and "state". It is worth noting in passing that one of the most original and instructive aspects of this research is its willingness to give a decisive role in this historical development to the mixing of the psychic and social planes under the heading of "processes of subjectivization".

Staying with Schmitt, though, it is not until his dark, ambitious geopolitical meditations in the post-war period, when the Eurocentric order now seemed to him gone forever, that we find any explicit allusion to one of the *real* conditions of modernization – an indication that is as sharp and clear as it is difficult to interpret. In his view, the entire modern order, or, as he put it, "the old *nomos* of the earth" (Schmitt 1950, p. 6), would emerge from the "legendary and unexpected discovery of a New World, an unrepeatable historical event. One can only think of a modern recurrence of such an event in fantastic parallels, such as that men on their way to the moon might discover a new and completely unknown planet" (ibid.).

Now, why was the stability of the modern order *in Europe* so dependent on the New World, and, more generally, on the imperialist expansion over the oceans and into the immense territories that lay beyond the borders of Europe? Schmitt's answer is that this extension of the political system to the whole surface of the earth meant an incisive "lightening of conflicts" (ibid.) between the European powers. One cannot say, however, that the answer is immediately clear, as when he was writing Schmitt knew perfectly well that, shortly after, that very dominion over the colonies would light the touch-paper of the most violent conflicts, which culminated in the Great War. In what sense can one speak, then, of a "lightening"? To understand his deeper meaning, we need first to look at the function of the so-called "amity lines", the geographical-political confines that for two centuries had officially marked the distinction between Old and New World:

> Beyond the line was an "overseas" zone in which, for want of any legal limits to war, only the law of the stronger applied … the line set aside an area where force could be used freely and ruthlessly … Everything that occurred "beyond the line" remained outside the legal, moral and political values recognized on this side of the line. This was a tremendous *exoneration* of the internal European problematic. The significance in international law of the famous and notorious expression "beyond the line" lies precisely in this exoneration.
>
> (Schmitt 1950, pp. 93–94)

In other words, the space "beyond the line" *embodies unlimited contingency*, the absolute negative that the new order was committed to expelling from the civilized world. Schmitt makes this identification so forcibly that he deliberately invokes Hobbes's *state of nature*, which is "a *no man's land*, but this does not mean it exists *nowhere*. It can be located, and Hobbes locates it, among other places, in the New World. In *Leviathan* the 'Americans' are an example of the wolf-character of men in the state of nature; and *Behemoth* refers to the atrocities committed by Spanish Catholics in the kingdom of the Incas" (Schmitt 1950, p. 96). In short, the *geographical* line distinguishing Old and New World absorbs and reproduces the *symbolic* border between order and disorder, signal and noise, protection and openness.

The exceptional symbolic value placed on the borderline between Old and New World could only make the *internal* borders in the European space less significant, although they were still *political* borders, which continued to separate those who might become enemies at any moment. In any case, the various European governments and peoples were now emissaries of the same civil order on the global scene, they participated in the same basic negation of disorder that was embodied in the sovereign, and they expressed this shared determination in the very act of recognizing each other as *justi hostes, legitimate* enemies, equally sovereign and with the right to defend their political identity by war. Legitimizing enmity paradoxically lightened it, and made agreements, limits and the regulation of conflicts plausible, on the premise that safeguarding the overall order was a shared interest and "burden" of all civilized peoples.

It is worth recalling that, subjectively, Schmitt gives no credit to colonialist mythology and loses no opportunity to remind us that concepts like "civilization" and "human rights" are usually the semantic correlative of the most savage wars of extermination. The coincidence in the "amity line" between a geographical border and a symbolic one was not, then, in any sense an objective fact, but a merely functional construct. Thanks to this coincidence, the "negation of disorder" carried out by the sovereign could again contain both exception and paradigm, but through a strategy that was diametrically opposed to that of ritual, in which only the *inclusion* of unlimited contingency made the existing order "sacred". Now, on the contrary, what legitimized order, what made it the *only* order possible, to the point of identifying it with the very idea of *civilization*, was the symbolic and geographical expulsion of an extreme possibility that seemed only a threat: the *internal* threat of the constituted order disintegrating, and the *external* threat of barbarism and disorder holding sway "beyond the line", where right was indistinguishable from violence. It is as a *synthesis of the Old and New World*, then, that modernity balanced the two demands and succeeded in neutralizing the anthropological paradox.

At bottom, the real form of this neutralization was thus much more complex and fragile than might appear at first sight. What the "line" claimed to divide was not just two geographical areas, but two phases of openness to the world that were inscribed with equal right in human nature: the state of nature and the civil state. In this symbolic value, however, the split that institutes the world remains paradoxical, neither more nor less than it was in archaic societies, as both the two poles have *unlimited* value, and are therefore able to absorb their opposite, thus dissolving the distinction (see Virno 2005). The "state of nature" is, in any case, *always* the bedrock on which sovereign authority rests, which can oppose it only on condition of placing itself on the same terrain and adopting its indistinct violence without hesitation and qualms, as the Spanish colonists cited in *Behemoth* showed. And, vice versa, to claim the status of a symbol of civilization as such and so "lighten" the intra-European conflicts, modern values had of necessity to be formulated in a *universalistic* logic – indifferent to any specific requisite of race, religion, class or gender – that was in strident contrast with the *national* character of the political institutions and with the separation between "barbarous" and "civilized" peoples, even though without that separation the overall equilibrium would inevitably crumble.

Modernity too, in short, was able to constitute itself as a "world" only on condition of coexisting with a latent paradox, which a complex and precarious political equilibrium could repress, but not wholly eliminate. The relative fusion between the symbolic and territorial aspects was one of the tools of this repression, which, obviously, made it no less precarious and provisory. Simply, now, for the first time, the "world" was *entirely situated in the real* and coincided with the extension of the planet, which had been carefully divided up by geographical-political borders.

Expelled from the social order, unlimited contingency still kept a structural hold over the *psychic* sphere, as a logical referent for any authentic demand for openness. The result was the need to transpose the sovereign decision *inside* the psyche, so that belonging to civilization would coincide with the infinite and painful task of repressing in it any legacy of the "state of nature". This is when the social control of the drives became an absolute social requirement, which no longer tolerated exceptions or counterweights, and dissociative behaviour was redefined as a dysfunctional and pathogenic psychic mechanism. Contingency now had to be fought, not only as a real danger, but also for its possible *attraction* on the psychic plane, dissolving the sovereign law in unlimited openness to the possible. The widespread "discontent of civilization", which was wholly unknown to ancient civilizations, the fascination of frontiers, social revolution, or simply war were so many collateral symptoms of this change of paradigm, which replaced the symbolic borders orchestrated by ritual with *real* barriers and borders, imposed by force of arms over the entire surface of the earth.

It is superfluous now to list all the abuse of power and all the illusions that for centuries have gone into solidifying these borders and the price paid for stopping them from crumbling away. The unavoidable question now is rather: what happens to the world when nothing can be done to stop them from crumbling away, and no one can delude himself any longer that symbolic paradoxes and conflicts can be kept behind real walls and borders?

Chapter 5

Anthropology of pluralism

> Die Philosophie ist eigentlich Heimweh,
> ein Trieb überall zu Hause zu sein.[1]
>
> Novalis, *Das allgemeine Brouillon*

I Worldlessness

The general reflections in the last few pages have taken us a long way from the specific terrain of contemporary forms of life. Yet, this summary anthropological exploration, ranging from archaic rituals to the internal ambivalence of modernization, was a necessary preliminary for tackling two kinds of problem that are highly relevant to the present world, and which have so far remained in the background.

The first unanswered question is whether our general model can somehow be confirmed empirically for the relations between social networks and psychic mechanisms, and thus take on a more tangible meaning. More generally, though, there is still the unanswered question of the value to give this model and the overall interpretation of the present in which to place it. We cannot ignore the fact that, in matters directly concerning the present, even the slightest shift of emphasis may be sufficient to direct thinking one way or another, and this wavering can become dramatic in the political sphere. So far we have got round this difficulty so as to remain as far as possible on a primary anthropological plane, but in the long run this choice risks muddying our thinking – even more so if we do not openly recognize the fact. To avoid this risk, my argument in this section aims to highlight the latent difficulties.

Specifically, I shall begin by suggesting that, at first sight at least, the underlying theme throughout this book – that there is a special bond between the forms of life in the present and dissociative behaviour – is by no means incompatible with some of the most widely accepted diagnoses of the crisis of modernity. So much so, that the slightest adjustment will confirm a whole set of ideas that have been widely followed in our culture and are now part of a broadly shared common

1 "Philosophy is really homesickness, the urge to be at home everywhere."

sense. The point is that, on further analysis, this first interpretation, which seems so simple and coherent, will inexorably prove inadequate, invalidated by aporias and internal limitations that, without wholly disqualifying it, effectively leave the thornier problems and more worrying overtones unclarified. Advancing beyond these limitations will require not only more work on the concepts, but, above all, an explicit detour into the minefield of *political* theory.

First, let us recall that dissociation seemed a defensive reaction to the overflow of contingencies, or, more precisely, to the *dissolution of the border between signal and noise* to which the human animal is exposed by virtue of our biological constitution. Let us imagine a situation in which, at least virtually, *everything* can have meaning, in which no certainty has foundation, and the most remote eventualities are sufficiently strong to confound any expectation. In such a case, marking out the field of the possible, establishing the confines of what is valuable and worth consideration, excluding and denying any aspect of the real that disturbs this reduction in complexity, would not be an arbitrary choice, but a vital necessity.

In normal conditions, though, the onus of this primary selection between order and disorder does not fall on the individual psychic system, which finds it already mapped out in the form of the *cultural world* inscribed in language, in the symbolic codes, and in the shared norms and expectations that define the identity of each specific culture. What sustains and articulates this "world" each time are *symbolic* operations, conveyed by communication signs and systems; but also, obviously, by *actual practices*, which effectively transform the environment, tending to make it ordered, foreseeable and *normal*, as no symbolic code and no system of norms could be successfully applied to absolute chaos. One might say that in each culture, what defines the perimeter of the world is precisely this interplay between symbolic norms and actual normality. Rooted within it, and therefore not required to institute *ex novo* the boundary between signal and noise, each individual may even risk stepping *outside* the boundary, thus making an original contribution to the development of their culture.

This, then, is, in every sense of the term, the *normal* situation. However, we may readily concede that the picture changes abruptly in crisis situations – what De Martino (1977) calls "cultural apocalypses". In these *exceptional* cases the whole symbolic system of a culture loses its capacity to organize the collective life, it can no longer filter the complexity of the environment, and leaves an impending sense of the "end of the world" as an extreme, but real, possibility. To ward off the threat, the symbolic order must be restored, starting from its exact opposite of disorder and unlimited contingency. In other words, the original indistinctness between signal and noise must be reproduced artificially in the closed perimeter of the ritual, and a *socially prescribed and regulated form of dissociation* takes on the task of restoring order to the world, so that the exceptional may end and normality return.

If we accept this underlying anthropological framework, we will easily be convinced that the basic problem of modernity derives from its inexorable tendency to dismantle every traditional symbolic order, to the point that cultural crises and apocalypses are *no longer the exception, but the rule.* Among the modern institutions, the capitalist economy, notoriously, has exacerbated this line of development more than any other: as it has expanded, it has demolished everywhere the fabric of customs, traditions and rites, which fixed the confines of each local culture and hampered the complete exploitation of the planet's resources and workforce. This rootlessness, which Marx had already denounced, became more and more marked during the twentieth century, along with the increasing pace of technical innovation, becoming the phenomenon of our time we have already referred to in passing – known in a significant strand of European culture, from Heidegger to Arendt, as *Weltlosigkeit*, or *absence of world.*

The basic idea is that individuals now live in a fluid context of perpetual change, governed by the ever more urgent rhythms of technical innovation, in which no tradition, no *custom* even, can any longer consolidate into a collective world, a stable framework of symbolic references and values that can ensure that experience has a communicable sense. This critical diagnosis was shared by much of the European philosophical elite as early as the mid-century. It has become almost a commonplace, now that some of the most macroscopic and controversial aspects of the current social system have become so evident: the planetary extension and computerization of the processes of production, freed of any spatial or temporal ties, and the growing *individualization* of producers and consumers, who belong less and less to their communities, but are catapulted into the contingency of the global market. Given these premises, nothing will seem more logical than also including in the general picture the dialectic between niches and micro-worlds presented earlier, which would mean deciding to consider it as a further aspect of the present condition of "absence of world", which may add to its incisiveness without changing its essential substance.

Actually, all that would be needed are a few marginal alterations to the account we have given so far – or, at least, so it seems. I have already mentioned that, in this interpretation, the emergence of disorder and unlimited contingency is no longer the sign of an exceptional crisis, but the normal condition by which social systems function. The incomprehensible, the "other", which the symbolic codes used to keep outside the confines of the "world", have now become a constituent part of daily life – but without ceasing to seem alien and disturbing. As a result, our ability to read the world depends on codes whose unreliability and inadequacy are confirmed every day. It is no surprise, then, that in extreme cases a defensive reaction may ossify these codes into "psychic retreats", designed to disavow an external complexity that can no longer be mastered and is therefore perceived as an annihilating threat to our identity. In this way the features of the dissociative personality are reproduced on the collective plane, and to illustrate with concrete examples this transition from the psychic to the social plane, we need only glance at the news reports of the last few years.

The most obvious example is the growing success throughout Europe of localist, anti-modern, authoritarian and xenophobic movements, all of which resort constantly to a mythology of identity and an *invention of traditions* lacking any historical reality. Outside Europe too, the tendency to construct cultural niches that offer protection from complexity seems to be strikingly testified everywhere by the overturning of classical nationalism, making splitting, rather than unification, the recurrent question today (Hobsbawm 1990). Just how far this claim to identity can translate into a disavowal of external reality is shown by the exemplary case of the "long-distance nationalists" cited by Benedict Anderson in an interesting addition to his classic study of "imagined communities" (see Anderson 1998, p. 58 ff). This term covers all those who are long-term residents in a geographical context that is far away from their country of origin, and model their cultural identity on this sense of their origins, exaggerating their idiosyncratic features, in opposition to the "foreign" world in which the whole of their actual existence is situated. On the other hand, in an environment that is now stripped of the customariness that made it a world, one need not be a migrant to look at the public dimension with a sense of estrangement and fear. Equally, the massive use of virtual reality and fiction, even when it does not amount to actual addiction, indicates a widespread need to avoid contact with external reality and retreat to a reassuring, painless niche, made up essentially of illusions.

Although the repudiation of the public sphere can be presented as a private, subjective choice, these examples suggest just how far dissociative behaviour, once it becomes widespread, will tend to become the target of social mechanisms specially designed to exploit their commercial, cultural or political potential in the most disparate forms. The denial of global reality may foment the political demand for security, but also offers a breeding ground for terrorism; the demand for illusions can give new strength to forms of traditional religious feeling, but also increase the turnover of the entertainment industry out of all proportion. Now, we need only suppose that mutual competitiveness drives these mechanisms to interconnect, and create ever more powerful and complex networks – as, indeed, happens – for us to find in the empirical fabric of present-day reality all the basic features of the dialectic between niches and micro-worlds, which we have so far described only in formal terms.

At this point we could take this line of interpretation further, with more detailed examples, but I think the general approach so far is sufficiently clear. In particular, while it does not coincide word for word with any specific theory, this description is effective because it can bring into a coherent framework suggestions and critical intuitions from various, opposing traditions that have all helped determine the "spirit of the age" with which Europe reflected on itself during and after the two great twentieth-century wars. Specifically, it combines Marxist anticapitalism with the denunciation of cultural decline that had been developing mainly in European conservative circles between the two wars. The diagnosis of *Weltlosigkeit*, conceived as a nihilistic drift that was inevitably inscribed in the mechanism of modernization, seems, in short, the central core on which these two opposing traditions tend to converge. That is probably why we found a more or less diluted form of this diagnosis in almost all the critical analyses, sociological descriptions, and even journalistic accounts of the problems of the present world.

The point now is whether this widespread consensus is already in itself a decisive argument, and whether, more generally, the picture we have just outlined actually responds to all the questions raised in the previous pages.

In my view, it does not. True, there is no shortage of empirical proof to back up this interpretation, although – as we shall now see – there is a certain amount of data for which the model we have just set out can only give a very rough explanation. However, the real difficulty is that these descriptive shortcomings are simply the sign of an inadequate use of those very concepts, such as "world" and "niche", that have been at the centre of our previous reflections. That is why, if we consider this conceptual scaffolding alongside the argument so far, we shall be forced to conclude that the whole model of interpretation actually needs radically correcting, and so even the aspects of empirical reality that seem to support it need to be re-interpreted in significantly different terms.

2 The limit and the unlimited

First, let us note that, in this picture, dissociative behaviour seems essentially to have only the dysfunctional, maladjusted value typical of forms of *denial* of external reality. Of course, it is acknowledged that this very denial makes it particularly suitable for interacting with certain social mechanisms, but only because these mechanisms seem *in turn* to be designed to deny reality in the form of escape, manipulation of consensus, or destructiveness pure and simple. If we take the correlation between the psychic and social dimensions as read, the interpretative model that emerges from the idea of "absence of world" tends in practice to repeat a stereotype of the modern Enlightenment that we have already discussed and dismissed as mere prejudice. That stereotype sees the act of isolating and separating a space of great symbolic value from the rest of the world – the act of "dissociating oneself" from the real and marking out a niche – as necessarily amounting to a *flight* from reality, and, therefore, the exact opposite of the authentic "world-forming" that a healthy culture should be fostering.

No one who accepts this premise is likely to conclude that in the global society of the present this repudiation of reality involves all subjects and social institutions to the same degree. At least virtually, a willingness to face the complexity of the world must also survive in some form or other: in supranational bodies, in the rules of communication, in the coherence of techno-scientific knowledge, or in the entrepreneurial imagination interested in exploiting to the full the potentiality and contingency of the market. It makes little difference which of these alternatives we adopt to give a name and face to the "positive" motor forces of present-day society. Either way, the denunciation of the absence of world impending on late modernity will effectively become an easy way of brushing aside pessimism by re-proposing a chain of antinomies with an all-too-modern flavour: openness to the world versus rejection of reality, progress versus reaction, civilization versus barbarism. However, our world is more and more ambiguous and many-sided, and so the hold these antinomies now have on it is weakening and they risk providing mere reassurance and propaganda.

Rather than its empirical ineffectiveness, though, the crucial question is its conceptual inadequacy. The clearest expression of this inadequacy is the unilateral way in which the "world" is described as a correlate of cultural reproduction: as a mere function of order, a guarantee of stability, and a protection from contingency, so that any factor of instability, surprise or openness to the indefinite logically falls on the side of *Weltlosigkeit*. As will be recalled, it was the inadequacy of an interpretative model of this kind that led us from the outset to concentrate on the veiled *paradox* implicit in any construction of a cultural world, given that the creative core of this activity always consists in distinguishing signal and noise, *starting from their indistinctness*. However, once the anthropological paradox is clearly visible, it becomes utterly improbable to think that the experience of the world modelled by a single culture – in the archaic as in the modern world – could ever really have been based on a simple opposition between order and chaos, the limit and the unlimited. Whatever strategies we adopt to neutralize the paradox, openness to the unlimited will always remain an essential part of being in the world, just as much as the desire to limit and reduce complexity. This, in turn, means that cultural order can only be established by articulating both desires together, reintroducing in practice the unlimited background *inside* the symbolic order that is called upon to deny it, and only in this way can it really assert itself as a "world".

In the previous chapter, the ritual of the *mundus* gave us a glimpse of the complex strategies by which a pre-modern culture could effectively model its specific openness to *the world as such* while keeping the social dimension and individual psychic resources in resonance, to the point of accepting without trauma or surprise the regular unleashing of contingency within the limits set up by the rite. Clearly, then, restricting the effectiveness of ritual to cases of "exceptional" emergency would be an improper simplification. Of course, the *mundus* of the Romans was only open three days in the year, but the ritual dimension covered the whole calendar of feast days, permanently fixing the paradigm for any profane activity. More generally, the effectiveness of rituality in absorbing the paradox is expressed precisely in the stable, foreseeable and *normal* form with which it inscribes the sacred in the profane, by which belonging to a world governed by ritual involves a *constant* attitude of dissociation, in phases of both stability and crisis. The fact is that once we accept the diagnosis of absence of world, we tend to interpret any experience of rootlessness, contingency and suspension of the rules in purely negative terms, even seeing it as unique to our period of crisis. In this way we risk projecting onto the archaic past, by contrast, the classicist illusion of a community happily and effortlessly rooted in its world, without contradictions.

We risk a similar underestimation, but one with more serious consequences, if, in the modern drive towards *universalism*, we insist on reading only the devastation of traditional communities, while missing the genuinely modern form in which the unlimited is reintroduced within the symbolic code. We have already mentioned in the previous chapter how, throughout the modern age, the nominal universality of values and rights has been one of the indispensable conditions for the *actual* confines between old and new world to overlap with the *symbolic* confines between civilization and a state of nature, thus absorbing its internal paradox. It was only thanks to this overlapping that modernity managed actually to constitute itself as a *world*, rather than being a mere cultural niche limited to North-Western Europe. On the other hand, this *Verweltlichung* of modernity was bound to take on a split, conflictual form, as, from the start, the universalism of values had clashed, virtually at least, with the dual system of confines that ensured the order of the world system: the borders between individual "civilized" nations and, deeper down, the dividing line between civilization and barbarism. There has probably been no episode in modern political history since the French Revolution that has not carried some trace of this unresolved tension. Its most emblematic expression, however, was the insistence with which the "civilized" nations regularly tried to deny access, beyond their confines, to those values and rights whose universal extension was the theoretical foundation of their claim to civilization.[2]

Of course, this classically modern contradiction between the universalism of abstract rights and the exclusiveness of actual privileges constantly appears in political theory, which has generally recognized it as the foundation for the standard dichotomy between "progressives" and "conservatives". We should note, however, that the most lucid and realistic European thinkers on both fronts of this dichotomy resolved the contradiction, though with diametrically opposed arguments and intentions. They theorized that, in practice, universalism has a merely cosmetic function, a purely logical and abstractly moral value, in the face of a political order in which the rights and freedoms of individuals remain rigidly bound to their being members exclusively of a free, sovereign nation-state.[3] With this logic Carl Schmitt, for example, underlines that the universality of human rights offers the perfect justification for a war of conquest, while Hannah Arendt sees the odyssey of refugees as reflecting the impotence of principled humanitarianism when it is not buttressed by the actual power of a state (see Arendt 1950, p. 267 ff). Now, it would be irresponsibly naive to brush aside such an undeniably coherent critical framework – one that, unfortunately, recent historical events seem to confirm in every detail. Yet, I think it is essential to recognize that this critical perspective fails

2 An exemplary case of this contradiction was the French revolutionary government's refusal to extend the rights of man to the colonized blacks in Haiti, whose rebellion the French put down with much bloodshed in 1802. At the time, Mirabeau asked the Assembly to remind the colonists that "in apportioning deputies according to the population of France, we have not taken into consideration horses and mules" (see Chatterjee 2004, p. 45). The notorious *Code noir* came back into force in the same year, authorizing and regulating the slave trade, which had previously been abolished by the Republican Convention in 1794. It remained in force until 1848, when slavery was finally abolished.

3 This is the sense of a famous phrase by Edmund Burke, who claimed to prefer his rights as an Englishman to the rights of man. The phrase is cited several times in Arendt (1950).

from the outset to give due credit to the interweaving of the limit and the unlimited, which generally marks the anthropological paradox, and, hence, cannot be reduced to superficial ideological window-dressing in modern society either. Even if we admit that, as yet, the modern system has not solved the tension between the two poles of the paradox, such a unilateral critical paradigm makes it difficult even to imagine a different expression of this dialectic, and, in practice, prevents us from grasping that, particularly *outside Europe*, it was universalism that encouraged the emergence of forms of life that are seeking new ways of healing the fracture.

3 The value of pluralism

In my view, the most suitable terrain for assessing the cost of this interpretative limit and evaluating the advisability of a change of direction is that provided by the debate on *pluralism* and the different values that the question acquired in the period both inside and outside Europe.

Today we are used to treating pluralism as a general concept that is substantially innocuous on the political plane. It is also identified with the coexistence of different parties, groups and cultures, and has come to be seen as a necessary – and therefore relatively insignificant – ingredient of any complex society. The truth is that this general "plural" character, which Aristotle had regarded as inscribed in the very idea of *polis*, has little to do with *political* pluralism in the strict sense, which began to take on clear contours only on the threshold of the last century. Considered in all its implications, pluralism was so far from being an obvious truism that, until yesterday, it was still a firmly rejected heresy in Europe, and, to a lucid analysis, is "still an experiment" that offers "no guarantees of meaning" (Walzer 1982, p. 27). As we shall see shortly, what makes the question so delicate is the fact that actual pluralism inevitably involves reintroducing the unlimited *inside* the political community, and it is therefore objectively incompatible with any attempt to solve the anthropological paradox by imposing a sharp division between order and disorder.

Once again, it is Schmitt who considers the question most lucidly and radically. An essay of 1930 specifically on this subject is devoted to demolishing the conceptions of political pluralism current at the time, in a series of arguments that reflect in exemplary fashion the most widespread attitude in Europe, despite the collective silence in which the essay was buried, for reasons easily understandable in the post-war period. Expressed in our terms, Schmitt's idea is that pluralism's essential aim is to revoke the horizontal split between the State and civil society, to the advantage of a system of vertical separations between social, religious or cultural groupings with equal dignity, so that "the state becomes a social group or association existing at best *side-by-side with*, but on no account above, the other associations" (Schmitt 1930, p. 153). According to Schmitt, the error in this perspective consists in believing that the political unity transferred to the state has its own content and can therefore exist *side by side with* cultural, religious unity and so on. The truth is that "the political has no specific substance" (ibid., p. 160), and marks only the degree of intensity, starting from which one or another of these unions/disunions – religious, cultural, economic or whatever – takes the extreme form of a distinction between enemy and friend. It is therefore precisely because it *has no* content of its own that the institution of the state can decide in a given situation what the actual effective unity of the people is, thus fixing in laws the situation and order which can be regarded as actual *normality*. In any case, a pluralist society cannot expect that the need to define the normal order will magically dissolve or resolve itself when it has ousted the state from its sovereign position. On the contrary, this need is exacerbated by the danger of the very plurality of the centres of power leading to the dismembering of political unity and civil war.

Against this extreme degeneration, the only suggestion the theoreticians of pluralism seem to make is to appeal to a *universalist* criterion against individual communities and identities that threaten to enter into conflict with each other: something like shared membership of "society" or humanity as such (Schmitt 1930, p. 153). However, according to Schmitt, a universal concept is the negation of any actual pluralism, as "Christians and Saracens, capitalists and proletarians, the good and the evil, the just and the unjust, delinquents and judges, are human beings, and with the help of such a universal concept, any distinction can be negated and any concrete community ruptured" (ibid., p. 162). The consequence is that criteria and values of this kind cannot ensure political unity precisely because they *do not exclude* either Christians or Saracens, proletarians or capitalists: they are not devised to discriminate, or, consequently, to really *decide*, when that is necessary. So, if the result is not simply a plunge into civil war, the system of vertical splits that the pluralist model puts in place of the sovereignty of the State will in fact be resolved in the dominion of various organized power groups. These will divide between them the spoils of the great Leviathan and force the citizenry into a painful moral balancing act to cope with the heterogeneous loyalties that are potentially hostile to each other and, in any case, unsuitable for fixing a permanent *normality*.

True, Schmitt was criticizing a political model rooted in the trade unionism of the Second International, in which what was being questioned was a plurality of organized centres of power, not of *cultures* in the real sense of the word. Indirectly, however, the criticism was also aimed at *cultural* pluralism, which in those very years began to take on a precise appearance, particularly in the United States. In this case, indeed, the contrast of viewpoints is still more strident, because "the substantial homogeneity of a nation" (Schmitt 1930, p. 156) remains for Schmitt the only authentic foundation of political unity. Having no substance of its own, the public sphere is constituted only when a people *decides* to place its identity in a particular substance, whatever it may be, thus committing itself to resisting as an *enemy* whatever threatens the unity that has been affirmed in this decision. What is essential, in short, is that the decision, like any boundary, necessarily has two faces: it includes something and *excludes* something else. In another work from this period, Schmitt advances the idea that the real core of *democracy* must consist in this political construction of the *demos*, and in the commitment to protect the unity of the people. It logically follows from this that "every real democracy [...] requires first homogeneity and second, if the need arises, the elimination or eradication of heterogeneity" (Schmitt 1926, p. 68).

Clearly, it is a very strange democracy that is constructed on such a rigid criterion of exclusion, and the reference to the "eradication of heterogeneity" sounds decidedly sinister with hindsight, in view of the Nazi methods of protecting a people's homogeneity, methods that were unfailingly endorsed by Schmitt a few years later. Yet, one cannot deny that, at bottom, Schmitt is simply drawing the logical consequences of two premises that are deeply rooted in European political culture. The first – that the unity of a republic rests on the homogeneity of the people – is traditionally linked with Rousseau's name. The second – that the only healthy pluralism is one between different national states, able to distinguish and recognize themselves and each other, thanks to the particular *homogeneity* that identifies each of them – was for centuries the key to European stability, effectively endorsed by the political choices of *all* the powers of the old continent. We shall need, then, to move *outside Europe* to find a configuration that is genuinely different, in which democracy and pluralism propose a different economy between the limit and the unlimited, and therefore an alternative answer to the anthropological paradox.

4 Creative democracy

Separating in this way the logical argument from polemics about the historical facts of the period, we can see that Schmitt's critique of pluralism is based on a general assumption: that defining a political community always starts by distinguishing between friend and enemy. This means it can never gather around a universal referent such as belonging to humankind or "society" in a global, all-embracing sense.

We cannot fully understand the meaning of this position if we do not take into consideration the anthropological vision it presupposes, which, in Schmitt (1932, p. 60), is expounded with explicit reference to Plessner (1931), but which is substantially shared by the whole of that area of German philosophy we have already referred to several times, from Gehlen to Heidegger. All these authors share the same basic intuition that, in itself, human nature does not involve a precise biological destiny, but only openness, the potentiality to make ours one or another of the many possible horizons of meaning that develop in various specific communities. In short, man is by nature only *his potential being*: this formula of Heidegger's re-expresses Aristotle's intuition of the intimately problematic nature of the "characteristic activity of a human being".

As we have already observed, it is the faculty of language that functions as a paradigm here – language, which is common to everyone only as *potentiality*, but can acquire actual existence only in a *specific* language, which distinguishes one specific culture from any other. Similarly, in politics membership of the human race remains, for each particular community, something potential and secondary that becomes ethically significant only for its value in a symbolic code and actual form of life, which is, by definition, *specific*, tracing a boundary and therefore distinguishing and reciprocally *excluding* "Christians and Saracens, capitalists and proletarians", and so on. There are just two logical outcomes to the appeal to universal rights and values, which pluralism seems unable to do without. One is for it to take on an ideological colouring, by which *one* specific community and *one* specific policy (for example, Anglo-American liberalism, according to Schmitt) assumes the right to dominate the others. Alternatively, it can announce a global process of *de-politicization*, in which all action is subjected to the imperatives imposed by technique, atrophying any human possibility of building one's world. The result, in this case, is absence of world, dissolving every form of life in a logic of pure biological survival, or, in Aristotle's terms, crushing every *bios* on a single *zoé*.

The disastrous outcome of anti-pluralist ideologies, which more or less explicitly appealed to this critical paradigm, is certainly not sufficient to demolish their coherence. This is shown by the fact that although this model has been excluded from official culture since the collapse of totalitarian ideologies, it has never ceased to exercise an influence, sometimes profound, on the most significant forms of critical thought that have arisen in Europe. Rather than wasting time dissociating ourselves from it, then, it would be useful if we could identify from within any possible blind spots it might have, reclaiming whatever truth it might have, cleansed of its misleading elements.[4] Now, the argument in the previous chapters has led us to suppose that the crucial question lies in the inevitably *paradoxical* nature that seems to mark the human condition, if only we examine closely the implicit premises in this anthropological perspective. In effect, though it was often touched on allusively, the founders of German philosophical anthropology never openly focused on this paradoxical aspect of the human condition. In authors such as Gehlen or Schmitt, indeed, there is a clear intention to solve the paradox in a sharp contrast between order and disorder, thus granting the institutions the single task of holding back contingency and expelling the unlimited from civil life. Even in Heidegger, who from the start had recognized openness to the indefinite as an essential feature of *Dasein*, this recognition was only effective ontologically and existentially, but *not* in the political sphere. I suggest that this complete or partial failure to transpose the anthropological paradox onto political terrain is the key to the problem, and has significantly impeded these theories from being absorbed, forcing them into a reductive and substantially "conservative" vision of late-modern phenomena.

At bottom, the problem concerns not so much the theories as the actual forms of organization of life. Precisely because we are faced with a *real* paradox, no theory can flatter itself that it is offering a solution to it, and it is the actual forms

4 For a courageous and incisive example of a critical reclaiming of Schmitt, see the essays collected in Mouffe (1999).

of life that have the delicate task of neutralizing it. This is what happened, though in profoundly different terms, both in the archaic appeal to the "sacred" and in the modern appeal to the universal value of "civilization". European culture seems to have been unable to respond adequately to the crisis of the latter paradigm – due to a combination of economic, social and geopolitical causes, on which theories have probably had little influence – and this failure in the *actual* forms of life is inevitably reflected on the plane of conceptual thinking too. In this respect, rather than highlighting the limits of a specific current of thought, the inability to transpose the complexity and paradoxes from the anthropological to the political plane, should be read as a sign of a deep-rooted inadequacy, which has to some extent involved the whole of the "old world". That is why modifying the conceptual system is not enough if we are to read more constructively the potentialities of democratic pluralism, but it would be useful to shift our attention to political development *outside Europe*.

The idea that the unity of the republic should correspond to a "substantial" homogeneity of the people long remained the dominant ideology in the United States too: the popular metaphor of the melting pot refers to a fusion of the various immigrant communities into a new homogeneous subject, exactly like the motto "*E pluribus unum*". Over time, however, the repeated waves of migration had transformed the vision of things to such a point that, by the end of the nineteenth century, "most Americans were 'hyphenated Americans' (Italo-Americans, Jewish Americans, etc.) ... more or less committed to their manyness. And pluralism was an alternative political program designed to legitimate this manyness and make it permanent" (Walzer 1990, pp. 595–596).

According to this account by Walzer, the first theoreticians of cultural pluralism – like Horace M. Kallen, who coined the famous definition of America as a "nation of nations" – had no intention whatsoever of questioning the political unity of the country, but simply of uncoupling it from its *cultural* identity: "their central assertion was that U. S. politics, as it was, did not require cultural homogeneity; it rested securely enough on democratic citizenship" (Walzer 1982, p. 11). Put briefly, the idea was that American citizenship should remain, in itself, something *anonymous*, in the interest of protecting the autonomy of political choices from the influence of one or another tradition, whether religious or "national" in the most restricted sense. For their part, these traditions were to be safeguarded in their plurality as an *ethical* heritage, to prevent a cultural identity based on the mere anonymous principle of citizenship withering into an abstractly formal criterion. The "hyphenated Americans", according to Kallen, were the perfect expression of this conjunction between political *anonymity* and cultural *specificity* (see Kallen 1924).

More than half a century later, however, Walzer had good reason to observe that the relation between the *political* and the *cultural* aspects – between the right-hand and left-hand sides of the "hyphen", so to speak – actually proved more complex than these theories suggested. Political citizenship did not, in fact, remain purely anonymous, but gave rise to an actual American identity with its own specific features, both culturally and ethically; but this identity was created *by removal* – given traditions taking second place to the individual's refusal to be reduced to any kind of collective belonging. So it was an ethic of singularity and of *mass migration* (see Walzer 1985), whose paradoxical outcome was that "a radical program of Americanization would *really* be un-American" (Walzer 1990, p. 610). At the same time, on the left-hand side of the "hyphen", traditional senses of belonging underwent a radical change, best exemplified by the many "reborn" communities in present-day America, which have to function as voluntary associations while being historical communities (Walzer 1985, p. 62), in the framework of a legal and social system that allows individuals both to escape their communities (through assimilation and mixed marriages) and a collective identity (ibid., p. 74).

It is clear that we are here at the antipodes of Schmitt's idea of "democracy" as a fusion between an "ethic of the state" and the cultural homogeneity of the "people". Yet, this pluralist model can boast a coherent link with the two founding moments of our own political history, to which Schmitt too had appealed. The first was the constitution of the *demos* in the archaic period, whose logical correlative was the *loosening* of tribal bonds and the consequent distinction between *ethnos* and *demos*, and the other was the foundation of the modern state as *neutral* towards the various religious affiliations. What is essential in this perspective is the fact that political identity is not constructed by *deciding* between communities in conflict, but by *negating* them. It does not represent the sovereignty of a group, a tradition or a culture, but rather the *unlimited contingency* that unites them all.

Building on this last aspect, we can return to the primary anthropological plane to re-read its political implications in terms that are completely overturned. As we have seen, in the picture outlined by philosophical anthropology, too, the "formation of a world" involved, deep down, a paradoxical interpenetration between the limit and the unlimited, between the protection of an *exclusive* symbolic order and openness to unlimited contingency. However, though this is recognized on the anthropological plane, the undefined and disturbing (literally, *un-heimlich*) side of openness to the world had been rigidly ejected from the political dynamic, where it might seem only to *threaten* the disintegration of the political community, on the *negation* of which both the people's identity and the sovereignty of the state should rest. By contrast, the pluralist model aims to transpose both sides of the primary anthropological paradox onto the political plane, though this means introducing a fracture, not only in the social body, but in individual identity itself, as is shown by the example of the "hyphenated Americans". To assume full citizenship, they need to *dissociate themselves*, partially at least, from their original identity; but, each time, this identity must wear the contingent clothes of a "reborn" community if it is not to become a desiccated universal abstract. This is not the pathetic balancing act Schmitt dismissed it as, but it is certainly a precarious exercise, performed on a tightrope of paradox, in which differences, *as differences*, must become so many examples of general human potentialities.

In 1939, in a speech written for his eightieth birthday – and read at the celebrations by Horace Kallen, no less, in its author's absence – John Dewey offered a clear and concise picture of this political ideal, defining it as *creative democracy* (see Dewey 1939). The adjective has an explicit anthropological connotation: it evokes the conviction, widespread in American pragmatism, that the basic feature of our humanity consists precisely in the *creative* faculty – the capacity to distinguish signal and noise, *starting from their indistinctness*, and that, therefore, indistinctness, contingency and general potentiality are the real deep motor-force of political life. It is hardly worth mentioning in passing that in modern culture this emphasis on creativity has tended to use forms of *successful dissociation*, of which play is the fundamental prototype, as convincing examples.

However antithetical it might seem to the European-style nation-state, we should note that this anthropological-political model imposed itself almost everywhere outside Europe as synonymous not only with modernity or democracy, but, above all, with *nationalism*, since, in countries like India or Indonesia, where dozens or hundreds of languages and cultures coexist, the appeal to the "nation" was bound to involve an immediate universalist connotation (see Chatterjee 2004). That is why nationalism could proceed for so long in perfect harmony with socialist internationalism in post-colonial cultures, to the point that Anderson (1998) recognized both as having the same logic of *unlimited seriality*, expressed in "such open-to-the-world plurals as nationalists, anarchists, bureaucrats and workers" (Anderson 1998, p. 29).

Of course, we cannot underestimate the profound difficulties inherent in such an elaborate project, combining anthropology and politics and starting from their shared paradoxical nature. It is, anyway, logically possible for the "unlimited" side to be resolved in an abstract universal – for the generally human *potentiality* to be unduly frozen in an actual identity, and therefore deployed *against* cultural formations, as a kind of pseudo-nature.[5] More generally, the threat of reducing the *bios* to the *zoé*, of political existence being subject to a logic of mere stewardship that reproduces and technically improves natural life does not disappear in this interpretative framework. However, logically, it acquires a sense that is the exact opposite of what Schmitt imagined and, more generally, of the critical paradigm of "absence of world". Rather than seeming the fruit of a dissociation that is inherent

5 The canonical example of this abstract universalism is the political use of *human rights* to justify the elimination of an enemy, defining him as an "enemy of humanity" – a question that, as we have already indicated, is developed by Arendt (1950) in a manner surprisingly close to Schmitt (1932). The confine between claiming creativity as a basic feature of human nature and this kind of abstract universalism can be very fine and take less predictable forms. Consider, for example, how Chomsky's linguistic research has recently been used to support the idea of "Mentalese", the hypothetical "language of thought", which is supposed to function as a *natural* foundation for all the various human languages. It is a theory with no empirical confirmation, from which Chomsky has always explicitly kept his distance. It crushes the delicate problem of linguistic creativity in the general exhibition of a biological precondition.

to the pluralist form of life, the threat now seems rather to come from the possibility of this delicate operation of dissociation, which should be rooted in individual identity no less than in collective institutions, coming up against possible *failure*. There remains only to understand, then, whether this failure, when it happens, is dictated by purely contingent causes, or is, in turn, hiding a structural root.

5 Politics and governmentality

In the same short essay in which he suggests including classical nationalism among the unlimited serialities that are open to the world, Anderson illustrates, on the opposite side, a "bound seriality, which has its origins in governmentality, especially in such institutions as the census and elections, exemplified by finite series like Asian-Americans, *beurs* and Tutsis" (Anderson 1998, p. 29). In this case, it is *statistical* calculation, introduced by the great censuses and repeated in electoral surveys, that conventionally fixes the logical requisites of the categories classified. These requisites are *exclusiveness* – one cannot be registered simultaneously as a Hutu and a Tutsi, even in cases where such a mixture is common – and *finite, numerable totality*, which requires an exact percentile for each group, as well as a precise distribution over the territory, however uncertain the methods of calculation may be.

This tends to create a kind of "bound seriality" that is the exact opposite of such open-to-the-world plurals as "workers" or "anarchists", which have their equivalent in every society on the face of the earth, and are therefore infinite in principle. The point is that while classical nationalism was modelled on those unbound plurals, contemporary nationalism, widespread among uprooted migrants and long-distance nationalists, adopted precisely this kind of closed seriality as its matrix, to the point of projecting the image of a "quasi-planetary dispersion of bounded identities" (Anderson 1998, p. 45), which inevitably reduces the idea of a nation to ethnicity.

If we now place this dialectic between limited and unlimited classifications in our anthropological framework, we might suppose that it is precisely the transition from one kind of classification to another that inverts the meaning of dissociative practices, which no longer encourage a social identity, open to the world, to emerge, but begin to make confines more rigid and, consequently, deny external reality. However, if we want to proceed along this path, we should try to fix at least some basic features of this dialectic between the political and the "governmental" plane, without which the whole system risks remaining incomprehensible and partial.

First, we should note that we are faced with a globally significant problem, which is particularly acute in ethno-nationalisms, but, at bottom, affects *all* present forms of life, whatever their social and geographical contexts. Not for nothing, the description of American pluralism above in Walzer (1982) brought out that even in America the gradual extension of the Welfare State has made inevitable some form of state recognition and the financing of at least those communities that were historically disadvantaged and otherwise risked being excluded from civil society. Just that, after a step of this kind, these communities are no longer organized as voluntary associations, but acquire some political roles, and even some civil rights (Walzer 1982), with the objective result of translating ethnic identity into an administrative classification (p. 23). The same argument leads Chatterjee (2004) to restate Anderson's categories, but reversing their sense: on a planetary scale, he notes, exclusion from civil society is a threat to the overwhelming majority of the world's population, to the point that universalist models maintain a show of credibility only in restricted, privileged areas, while a programme of authentic democratization necessarily involves "dirty[ing] one's hands in [...] the politics of governmentality" (Chatterjee 2004, p. 39).

Unsurprisingly, Chatterjee appeals quite explicitly here to Foucault's later research – already implicit in his choice of the term "governmentality", which makes the general perspective of the problem still broader and more articulated. Since 1978 at least,[6] Foucault had been trying to reconstruct the history of technologies designed for the "government of self and others", which initially developed in the forms of the Church's "pastoral" power, and, in the modern world, would inevitably insinuate themselves deeper and deeper into the emerging techniques of government, finally finding their natural outlet in political economy (see Foucault 1978, 1979). The most specific feature of these techniques of government seems to be their propensity to bypass ways in which *political power* in the strictest sense is applied. Of course, their ultimate aim, as we have said, is the government of *human beings* – but "human beings" considered not as subjects of rights, but as mere *living beings*, singled out in the exercise of their biological functions of health, nutrition and reproduction. Consequently, the target of the new technologies is not "peoples", but *populations*, which are analysed, measured and governed on the basis of a cost-benefit calculation whose ideal parameters – security, prosperity and well-being – claim substantial political neutrality.

As we can see, what is at stake here are the same features of "neutralization and depoliticization" that, in early twentieth-century European ideology, from Schmitt to Heidegger, made up the extreme threat of "absence of world", which was a result of *bios* finally being reduced to *zoé*. However, the basic points of this paradigm are now completely overturned.

To begin with, Foucault uses many arguments to show that the emerging late-modern "governmentality" did not actually develop in two different stages, as Schmitt had suggested, first submitting to the sovereignty of the State and only at some later point asserting itself *against* it. In short, the idea that the European political model suddenly found itself threatened by the dehumanizing dominion of technique – with liberal capitalism the most coherent expression of it – now seems, in the light of the facts, a groundless simplification. On the contrary, the relation

6 Foucault himself noted this change, although many hints were already present in his previous courses and writings. In what follows I therefore refer mainly to Foucault (1978, 1979).

between political sovereignty and technology of government has been so much more complex and turbid from the start that the premises of the modern political system – homogeneous populations and a balance between the national powers – are actually one of the first fruits of the governmental machine (see Foucault 1978). So, when the neo-liberal project of founding the legitimacy of political power on the effectiveness of governmental action began to emerge between the two wars, this inversion of the relations between politics and economics had every right to present itself as a coherent development, and not as a subversion of the power relations that had previously been reflected in the ethic of the State. Above all, it was not pluralism that dictated the agenda of this development, but, if anything, the gradual emptying of it in favour of governmental practices designed, by definition, for closed groups, countable identities and exclusive memberships.

On these premises, the illusion that an appeal to the homogeneity of a people might constitute a dyke or counterweight to these power practices clearly derived from the naive conviction that the parameters and technologies that were entrusted with the government of life, deep down really expressed a politically *neutral* motive – menacing and dehumanizing, but independent and averse to political power. Actually, wherever it sets down roots, governmental calculation tends to generate processes of inclusion/exclusion extremely similar to that "eradication of heterogeneity" that Schmitt regarded as an inevitable corollary of political decisions, with the sole difference that this decision now becomes all the more anonymous and hidden, the more it is able to penetrate the deep tissue of biological life. So it is the drive for pluralism that must resist this penetration, tearing the veil of its supposed neutrality and initiating practices of *democratization* that can modify the governmental machine from within or stop it from functioning.

Logically, there is a significant variety of strategies of this kind, and how effective they are is a matter of opportunity and contingency that does not change the general picture. What is essential is that, in any actual encounter or negotiation, the meeting between the universalism of political motives and the specifics of governmental practices is the real acid test of the pluralist project to transpose the paradoxical duality of openness to the world wholly into the political dimension. This must be done in such a way that will safeguard both the autonomy of each individual cultural niche and their reciprocal transitivity, and ensure the same dignity to each segment as well as the right of individuals to dissociate, if they wish, from any collective membership. At this point, not only the coherence of the pluralist project, but the future of politics in general, depends on ensuring that these demands can coexist while maintaining their inner tension. It is a matter of understanding whether the emergence of the primary anthropological dimension, which the new techno-sciences seem to make inescapable, must inexorably oblige any political experience to submit to the optimized reproduction of the natural life, as the whole of European philosophical anthropology has taught us to fear. Or can it disclose the conditions of a different public sphere, in which a fluid, creative network of distinctions and differences shoulders most of the responsibility of political decision-making, without recourse to a horizontal split between society and the State? If it is in these terms that humanity in the present must deal with the anthropological paradox, presumably only a psychic identity that has learnt to coexist with its possible forms of splitting can offer a positive contribution to this challenge.

To truly grasp its internal complexity, the dialectic between niches and micro-worlds should therefore be read as a recent stage in this development, one probably set off by the gradual adaptation of the government machine to a new technological standard, which, significantly, was until recently designated with a term – *cybernetics* – whose etymology is related to control and government. This is, presumably, the reason why, in our description of the present situation, two aspects that Foucault had already focused on several decades earlier have emerged so insistently. The first: that the interconnectedness of politics and governmentality is linking the social systems more and more closely to psychic mechanisms, to the point of constituting individual identity. The second: that what is taking form in this process is a new field of conflicts and tensions, in which dangers and horrors are certainly rising to the surface, but also new possibilities of resistance and creative definition of life.

Whether one inclines to pessimism or optimism in a dilemma of these proportions naturally remains an arbitrary choice of little significance. In conclusion, however, we may want to reconsider the gloomier diagnoses announcing a world doomed to dehumanization if we are aware that the tension between the limit and the unlimited, and between the need to take refuge in a niche and the desire to explore external contingency, is not a challenge that humanity is facing for the first time. Everything, indeed, suggests that this challenge expresses a paradox that the human animal has already had to face in the decisive moments of its sojourn on earth.

Bibliography

Agamben, G. 1995 *Homo sacer*, Torino: Einaudi (*Homo Sacer: Sovereign Power and Bare Life*, Stanford CA: Stanford University Press, 1998).

Anderson, B. 1991 *Imagined Communities*, London-New York: Verso.

Anderson, B. 1998 *The Spectre of Comparisons*, London-New York: Verso.

Arendt, H. 1979 [1950] *The Origins of Totalitarianism*, San Diego: Harcourt Brace Jovanovich.

Austin, J. 1975 [1962] *How to Do Things with Words*, London: Oxford University Press.

Bell, C. 1992 *Ritual Theory, Ritual Practice*, Oxford-New York: Oxford University Press.

Benasayag, M. and Schmit, G. 2003 *Les passions tristes. Souffrance psychique et crise sociale*, Paris: La Découverte.

Benjamin, W. 1974–1989 [1940] Über den Begriff der Geschichte, in Id., *Gesammelte Schriften*, I (2), Frankfurt a. M.: Suhrkamp (trans. in *Selected Writings*, Vol. 4, Cambridge MA: Belknap Press, 2003).

Benveniste, É. 1966 [1963] La philosophie analytique et le langage, in Id., *Problèmes de linguistique générale*, vol. I, Paris: Gallimard (trans. in *Problems in General Linguistics*, Coral Gables: University of Miami Press, 1971).

Boltanski, L. and Chiapello, E. 2000 *Le nouvel esprit du capitalisme*, Paris: Gallimard (*The New Spirit of Capitalism*, London-New York: Verso, 2005).

Bromberg, P. 1996 *Standing in the Spaces*, Hillsdale NJ: Analytic Press.

Burkert, W. 1998 *The Creation of the Sacred*, Cambridge MA: Harvard University Press.

Caretti, V. and Di Cesare, G. 2005 Psicodinamica delle dipendenze, in V. Caretti and D. La Barbera (ed.), *Le dipendenze patologiche*, Milano: Cortina, pp. 11–32.

Chatterjee, P. 2004 *The Politics of the Governed*, New York: Columbia University Press.

De Carolis, M. 2004 *La vita nell'epoca della sua riproducibilità tecnica*, Torino: Bollati-Boringhieri.

De Carolis, M. 2017 *Il rovescio della libertà*, Macerata: Quodlibet.

De Martino, E. 1977 *La fine del mondo*, Torino: Einaudi.

De Mauro, T. 1963 *Storia linguistica dell'Italia unita*, Bari: Laterza.

Dennett, D. 1990 Cognitive Wheels: The Frame Problem of AI, in M.A. Boden (ed.), *The Philosophy of Artificial Intelligence*, Oxford-New York: Oxford University Press, pp. 147–170.

Dewey, J. 1988 [1939] Creative Democracy. The Task Before Us, in Id., *Later Works of John Dewey*, Carbondale: Southern Illinois University Press.

Dreyfus, H.L. 1981 From Micro-Worlds to Knowledge Representation: AI at an Impasse, in J. Haugeland (ed.), *Mind Design*, Cambridge MA: The MIT Press, pp. 161–204.

Ehrenberg, A. 1998 *La fatigue d'être soi*, Paris: Odile Jacob.
Esposito, R. 2006 *Terza persona*, Torino: Einaudi (*The Third Person*, Cambridge: Polity Press, 2012).
Fodor, J. 1981 Methodological Solipsism Considered as a Research Strategy in Cognitive Psychology, in J. Haugeland (ed.), *Mind Design*, Cambridge MA: The MIT Press, pp. 307–338.
Fonagy, P. and Target, M. 1996 and 2000 Playing with Reality, in *International Journal of Psycho-Analysis* 1996 (I and II) and 2000 (III).
Foucault, M. 2004 [1978] *Sécurité, territoire, population*, Paris: Gallimard-Seuil (*Security, Territory, Population*, Basingstoke and New York: Palgrave Macmillan, 2007).
Foucault, M. 2004 [1979] *Naissance de la biopolitique*, Paris: Gallimard-Seuil (*The Birth of Biopolitics*, Basingstoke and New York: Palgrave Macmillan, 2008).
Freud, S. 1968 [1896] Zur Ätiologie der Hysterie, in *Gesammelte Werke*, vol. 1(4), Frankfurt a. M.: Fischer (The Aetiology of Hysteria, in *The Standard Edition of the Complete Psychological Works of S. F.*, London: The Hogarth Press and the Institute of Psycho-Analysis, 1955–1964, vol. 3).
Freud, S. 1927 Die Zukunft einer Illusion, in *Werke*, cit. vol. 14, pp. 323–380 (The Future of an Illusion, in *The Standard Edition* cit., vol. 21).
Freud, S. 1927b Fetischismus, in *Werke*, cit. vol. 14, pp. 309–318 (Fetishism, in *The Standard Edition*, cit., vol. 21).
Freud, S. 1929 Das Unbehagen in der Kultur, in *Werke*, cit. vol. 14, pp. 419–506 (Civilization and its Discontents, in *The Standard Edition*, cit. vol. 21).
Freud, S. 1938 Die Ichspaltung im Abwehrvorgang, in *Werke*, cit., vol. 17, pp. 57–62 (Splitting of the Ego in the Process of Defense, in *The Standard Edition*, cit. vol. 23).
Freud, S. 1938b Abriss der Psychoanalyse, in *Werke*, cit., vol. 17, pp. 63–138 (An Outline of Psycho-Analysis, in *The Standard Edition*, cit. vol. 23).
Galli, C. 1996 *Genealogia della politica. Carl Schmitt e la crisi del pensiero politico moderno*, Bologna: Il Mulino.
Gehlen, A. 1966 [1940] *Der Mensch. Seine Natur und seine Stellung in der Welt*, Frankfurt, a. M.: Athenäum (8) (*Man: His Nature and Place in the World*, New York: Columbia University Press, 1988).
Goldberg, A. 1999 *Being of Two Minds*, London: The Analytic Press.
Goldberg, P. 1995 "Successful" Dissociation, Pseudovitality and Inauthentic Use of the Senses, in *Psychoanalytic Dialogues*, vol. 5, no. 3, pp. 493–510.
Goodman, N. 1951 *The Structure of Appearance*, Cambridge MA: Harvard University Press.
Goodman, N. 1956A World of Individuals, in I.M. Bochenski, A. Church and N. Goodman (ed.), *The Problem of Universals: A Symposium*, Notre Dame IN: University of Notre Dame Press, pp. 13–31.
Grilliat, D. 1999 *La Spaltung: scission, coupure, clivage, division*, Lille: ANRT.
Habermas, J. 1981 *Theorie des kommunikativen Handelns*, Frankfurt a. M.: Suhrkamp (*The Theory of Communicative Action*, Boston: Beacon Press, 1984).
Hacking, I. 1995 *Rewriting the Soul*, Princeton: Princeton University Press.
Haugeland, J. (ed.) 1981 *Mind Design*, Cambridge MA: The MIT Press.
Heidegger, M. 1983 [1930] Die Grundbegriffe der Metaphysik, in Id., *Gesamtausgabe*, vol. 29–30, Frankfurt a. M.: Klostermann (*The Fundamental Concepts of Metaphysics*, Bloomington IN: Indiana University Press, 2008).

Heidegger, M. 1998 [1934] Logik als die Frage nach dem Wesen der Sprache, in Id., *Gesamtausgabe*, vol. 38, Frankfurt a. M.: Klostermann (*Logic as the Question Concerning the Essence of Language*, Albany NY: Suny Press, 2009).

Heidegger, M. 1950 [1936] Der Ursprung des Kunstwerkes, in Id., *Holzwege*, Frankfurt a. M.: Klostermann (*Off the Beaten Track*, Cambridge: Cambridge University Press, 2002).

Hobsbawm, E.J. 1990 *Nations and Nationalism since 1780*, Cambridge: Cambridge University Press.

Humphrey, N. and Dennett, D.C. 1998 Speaking for our Selves, in D.C. Dennett, *Brainchildren*, Cambridge MA: Bradford.

Joas, H. 1992 *Die Kreativität des Handelns*, Frankfurt a. M.: Suhrkamp (*The Creativity of Action*, Chicago: University of Chicago Press, 1996).

Kallen, H.M. 1924 *Culture and Democracy in the United States*, New York: Boni & Liveright.

Kant, I. 1902 [1784] Ideen zu einer allgemeinen Geschichte in weltbürgerlicher Absicht, in Id. *Gesammelte Schriften*, Berlin: Akademie-Ausgabe.

Kant, I. 1787 Kritik der reinen Vernunft, in Id. *Gesammelte Schriften*, cit.

Lorenz, K. 1999 La formazione filogenetica e storico-culturale dei riti, in *Natura e destino*, Milano: Mondadori, pp. 161–186.

Luhmann, N. 1984 *Soziale Systeme*, Frankfurt a. M.: Suhrkamp (*Social Systems*, Stanford CA: Stanford University Press, 1995).

Lyotard, J.F. 1979 *La condition postmoderne*, Paris: Minuit (*The Post-Modern Condition*, Manchester: Manchester University Press, 1984).

Malik, K. 2013 *Multiculturalism and its Discontents*, Kalkata-London: Seagull Books.

Mannoni, O. 1969 *Clefs pour l'Imaginaire*, Paris: Seuil.

Marramao, G. 1994 *Cielo e terra. Genealogia della secolarizzazione*, Roma-Bari: Laterza.

Montani, P. 2007 *Bioestetica*, Roma: Carocci.

Mouffe, Ch. (ed.) 1999 *The Challenge of Carl Schmitt*, London-New York: Verso.

Pandolfi, M. 1997 L'altro sguardo e il paradosso antropologico, in H. Bhabha (ed.), *Nazione e narrazione*, Roma: Meltemi, pp. 9–26.

Plessner, H. 1931 *Macht und menschliche Natur*, Berlin: Junker und Dünnhaupt.

Pruyser, P.W. 1991 [1985] Forms and Functions of the Imagination in Religion, in H.N. Malony and B. Spilka (ed.), *Religion in Psychodynamic Perspective*, Oxford-New York: Oxford University Press, pp. 170–188.

Rappaport, R. 1999 *Ritual and Religion in the Making of Humanity*, Cambridge UK: Cambridge University Press.

Rosier-Catach, I. 2004 *La parole efficace. Signe, rituel, sacré*, Paris: Seuil.

Schechner, R. 1987 The Future of Ritual, in *Journal of Ritual Studies* vol. I, no. 1.

Schmitt, C. 1934 [1922] *Politische Theologie*, Berlin: Duncker u. Humblot (2nd ed.) (*Political Theology*, Chicago: Chicago University Press, 2005).

Schmitt, C. 1994 [1926] Der Gegensatz von Parlamentarismus und moderner Massendemokratie, in Id., *Positionen und Begriffe*, Berlin: Duncker u. Humblot (3rd ed.), pp. 60–74.

Schmitt, C. 1930 Staatsethik und pluralistischer Staat, in Id., *Positionen und Begriffe*, cit., pp. 151–165.

Schmitt, C. 1963 [1932] *Der Begriff des Politischen*, Berlin: Duncker & Humblot (*The Concept of the Political*, Chicago: University of Chicago Press, 1996).

Schmitt, C. 1974 [1950] *Der Nomos der Erde*, Berlin: Duncker & Humblot (2) (*The Nomos of the Earth*, New York: Telos Press, 2003).

Schreiber, F.R. 1973 *Sybil*, Chicago: Regnery.
Sloterdijk, P. 1999 [1998–2004] *Sphären*, Frankfurt a. M.: Suhrkamp.
Spanos, N.P. 1996 *Multiple Identities and False Memories: A Sociocognitive Perspective*, Washington DC: American Psychological Association.
Steinberg, M. and Schnall, M. 2001 *The Stranger in the Mirror*, New York: HarperCollins.
Steiner, J. 1993 *Psychic Retreats*, London: Routledge.
Tambiah, S.J. 1985 *Culture, Thought and Social Action*, Cambridge MA: Harvard University Press.
Turner, V. 1986 *The Anthropology of Performance*, New York: Paj Publications.
Uexküll, J. von 1956 [1934] *Streifzüge durch die Umwelten von Tieren und Menschen*, Hamburg: Rohwolt.
Virno, P. 2005 Il cosiddetto "male" e la critica dello Stato, in *Forme di vita*, no. 4, DeriveApprodi, Roma, pp. 9–36.
Walzer, M. 1982 Pluralism in Political Perspective, in *The Politics of Ethnicity*, Cambridge MA/London: Harvard University Press.
Walzer, M. 1985 *Exodus and Revolution*, New York: Basic Book Inc.
Walzer, M. 1990 What Does it Mean to Be an "American"?, in *Social Research*, vol. 57, no. 3.
Winnicott, D.W. 1971 *Playing and Reality*, London: Tavistock Publications.
Wittgenstein, L. 1922 [1921] *Tractatus logico-philosophicus*, London: Routledge and Kegan Paul.
Wittgenstein, L. 1964 [1930] *Philosophische Bemerkungen*, Oxford: Blackwell.
Wittgenstein, L. 1953 [1947] *Philosophische Untersuchungen*, Oxford: Blackwell.

Index

For Product Safety Concerns and Information please contact our EU representative GPSR@taylorandfrancis.com
Taylor & Francis Verlag GmbH, Kaufingerstraße 24, 80331 München, Germany

www.ingramcontent.com/pod-product-compliance
Ingram Content Group UK Ltd.
Pitfield, Milton Keynes, MK11 3LW, UK
UKHW011020180926
475701UK00004B/847
* 9 7 8 0 3 6 7 3 4 8 9 2 2 *